ON THE
GREEK STYLE

ON THE GREEK STYLE

Selected Essays in Poetry and Hellenism

by GEORGE SEFERIS

Translated by REX WARNER *and*
TH. D. FRANGOPOULOS
With an Introduction by REX WARNER

DENISE HARVEY (PUBLISHER) • LIMNI, EVIA, GREECE

First published in the United States of America in 1966
by Atlantic-Little, Brown
and in Great Britain in 1967
by The Bodley Head

Reprinted in 1982, 1992 and 2000 by Denise Harvey (Publisher)
340 05 Limni, Evia, Greece

Copyright © Maro Seferiadis 1982
English translation copyright © Rex Warner 1966
All rights reserved
Printed in Greece
ISBN 960-7120-03-5

Cover photograph:
George Seferis at the Theatre of Dionysos, Athens, 1965
(courtesy of the National Bank Cultural Foundation and Anna Londou)

Cover design by Anna Katsoulaki

On the Greek Style is the fifth publication in
THE ROMIOSYNI SERIES

Introduction

THE history of modern Greece and of the specifically modern Greek language and literature is both interesting and unique. No other language has so long a tradition. A writer of today will find himself using words and phrases which were in use long before Homer. And through all the vicissitudes of so extensive a history, the tradition is continuous. As Seferis will often point out, a modern Greek folk song may throw light on a passage of Homer or of Aeschylus. I doubt too whether it is possible to find a better guide than Thucydides to modern Greek politics. And of course this tradition, peculiarly Greek as it is, is also in a sense common to humanity. So far as human values are concerned no tradition in history is of comparable importance.

It is a tradition that has seldom or never been static. Even the gods are capable of change, yet they are the same gods. So the Greeks themselves and their language have suffered change but never a loss of identity.

Particularly to be noted are the events of the last one hundred and fifty years. For four hundred years (from 1453) Greece was under the subjugation of the Turks. The consciousness of a long and proud

ON THE GREEK STYLE

tradition had never been lost, but with the recovery of political independence the necessity for in some way defining this tradition and for expressing it in the modern language became urgent. Dissensions and discussions as deep, and often as bitter, as those that in ancient times found expression in the war between Athens and Sparta began to appear not only in politics but among literary men, philosophers and linguists. As late as 1945 it was possible to argue (though of course there was no sense in the argument) that a writer who chose to employ in his work the living speech of the people rather than an artificial and puristic language was likely also to be dangerous politically — and this in spite of the fact that modern Greek writers, almost without exception, had for many years turned their backs on the artificial and chosen the real.

However, even though the main battle, in spite of protests from a reactionary minority, had been won, much remained to be done in this present generation in the way not only of consolidation but of exploration. The problem of style, of finding the precise expression appropriate to the writer's own insight, to his tradition and to the air which he breathes, is, of course, a problem which must be faced by every writer in every country; but in Greece, which is not only very old but also very new, the problem has been and has been seen to be one of very special urgency and complexity. And Seferis does not exaggerate when he writes: "Expression in the modern Greek language has been the main concern of my whole life."

Seferis's poetry is, of course, well known and has been influential not only in Greece but throughout the world. But in Greece he is also well known as a prose writer, and in prose his work has been influential both as regards its matter or argument and as regards its manner or style. Here too he has based himself on the rhythms of actual modern Greek speech, and so far as this aspect of his work is concerned, it is obviously impossible to reproduce in translation what is novel in the original. The theory behind his practice is, however, clearly stated in essay after essay — particularly clearly, perhaps, in the *Dialogue on Poetry* with its subtitle *What Is Meant by Hellenism?* Over and over again he insists that Hellenism, the Greek style, is not a drowned body to be revived by artificial respiration administered by professors and academicians. It is alive today and is intimately connected with the past of Homer, of Pericles, of Alexander and of Byzantium. The "race" (a word that has nothing to do with the "racism" of Hitler or of Alabama) has recovered its independence, but has always persisted even in subjugation. And, though no one has a greater love and respect for the classics and for culture in general than Seferis, he is utterly and invariably opposed to any suggestion that the culture of his land (or of any land) is the property of a caste whose task it is to "educate" the rest in an imitation of past greatness. "Popular education," he writes, "is concerned not only with how we should teach the people, but with how we should learn from the people." Or again: "If we want to understand the ancient Greeks, it is always into the soul of our own people that we should look."

This is not mere nationalism. It is a statement of fact. But if this statement is exaggerated, if it is maintained that nothing is of value unless it is specifically "Greek," that any influence which can be called "foreign" is to be deplored, Seferis, who is a European as well as a Greek, will be the first to object and to point out that such views also are artificial, abstract and puristic.

It will be clear, I think, even from the present selection, chosen from a much greater volume of essays, that Seferis's literary theory is not only illuminating but consistent. He often says of himself, "I keep on saying the same things." So do most great writers. On the other hand, he would not claim to have written a complete and exhaustive study of aesthetics. Even had he intended such a project, the exigencies of his life as civil servant, diplomat and poet would have prevented its completion. In a career of thirty-eight years the longest holiday he has had was one of two months. During this time he composed his poem "The Thrush."

Much of his work in prose, then, has been occasional. The opening of an exhibition in Athens provided him with an opportunity to express his

INTRODUCTION

admiration, felt for many years, for the work of the painter Theophilos; the death of his old friend Sikelianos prompted an affectionate tribute to that great poet; a lecture given to the Greeks in Egypt during the dark days of the war was an appropriate occasion to recall Makryannis, the hero of the War of Independence. Yet however different the occasion, he is always, in a variety of ways, "saying the same things." One will admire his subtlety, but still more his perfect integrity.

The Greek title for his collected essays is ΔΟΚΙΜΈΣ (*Dokimés*), a variation from the accepted modern Greek word for "essay," which is *dokímio*. The word chosen by Seferis has rather the old meaning of "essay" in English — "attempt" — than the newer meaning of "study" or "dissertation." In his preface to the second Greek edition of *Dokimés* he writes: "Words have also their stubborn fate. When I first chose the title *Dokimés* I had in mind the meaning of the word 'essay' (*dokímio*), though wishing to express something freer and fresher, but now as I glance at the present book, I notice that the title insists on having its usual meaning of an attempt, or of a work about which we are never certain whether or not it will be concluded."

It should be added that the selection of essays here translated is only a small portion of Seferis's prose work — rather less than half of those published in the first volume of his collected essays (the second volume is shortly to be published in Athens). They have been selected by him as representative of his work, and were he to go on writing volume after volume it seems to me likely that his essay in criticism will never be concluded in any hieratic or rigid sense. He has this in common with his countryman Socrates — that, being perfectly certain of some things, he is also aware of horizons that extend beyond the view of the legislator. As a poet he is aware not only of the power and sanctity of words, but also of their limitations. As a Greek he knows that every excess, whether it takes the form of an arrogant flamboyance or of a dictatorial rigidity, will inevitably be punished by those ministers of justice the Erinyes. And in our days, when so much of criticism is devoted to a kind of dissection, his insistence that literature exists only when it is alive and breathing may be of particular value.

REX WARNER

Contents

	Introduction	v
I.	Theophilos	1
II.	Sikelianos	13
III.	Makryannis	23
IV.	Antoniou: Our Seafaring Friend	67
V.	Dialogue on Poetry: What Is Meant by Hellenism?	73
VI.	Letter on "The *Thrush*"	99
VII.	The *Thrush*	107
VIII.	Cavafy and Eliot — A Comparison	119
IX.	Letter to a Foreign Friend	163
X.	On a Phrase of Pirandello	183
XI.	Art in Our Times	191

I
Theophilos

ONCE upon a time, as they say, a baker commissioned a poor painter to paint a picture of him taking loaves of bread out of the oven. The painter started on his work, and when he came to putting in the baker's rake, instead of following the laws of perspective and making it horizontal, he drew it perpendicular, showing the whole breadth of its surface; then, in the same way, he drew a loaf of bread on the rake. A clever man came past and said to the painter, "That loaf of bread is going to fall down, the way you've painted it." Without bothering to turn his head, the painter replied, "Don't worry. Only real loaves fall down; the painted ones stay put, and in a picture one ought to show everything."

This story reminds me of that great artist who, just because "in a picture one ought to show everything," when he was painting the view of Toledo omitted from his panorama in the name of art the Hospital of Don Juan Tavera, but put it in separately on a map. That artist, of course, was the Cretan Domenicos Theotocopoulos, or "El Greco";

This speech was made at the opening of the first exhibition of the painter's work (British Institute, Athens, May 2, 1947). At that time Theophilos was recognized by only a very small circle of admirers. In August 1965 a museum entirely dedicated to his work was opened at his birthplace, the island of Mytilene. (EDITOR'S NOTE: All footnotes are by the author unless otherwise indicated.)

and the painter in the story about the loaves was Theophilos G. Hajimihail from Mytilene, "formerly chieftain and door guard in Smyrna."

There is no impiety in my parable. The important distinction to make is not between the very great craftsmen and the lesser ones (that would be to proceed like an encyclopedist or a Baedeker); the real distinction is between those who have brought to the lighthouse of art even a small drop of oil and those who are by nature of no interest to art at all. What we look for is not who is a great and who is a minor artist, but who keeps art alive. Now, one of those very few people whom I see as a source of life for our contemporary painting is Theophilos. His loaves of bread did not fall down; they "stay put," as he said; they stay put and they are nourishing.

We therefore owe a deep debt of gratitude to those who from the very beginning had the ability to recognize and the virtue to devote themselves to this despised work and to preserve it as best they could. We should be grateful too to those who had the initiative to collect in these rooms for this first public appearance the best paintings of Theophilos that are still in Athens (there has been a large collection of them in Paris for some years). In more favorable circumstances it might have been possible to find a permanent home for this heritage left by Theophilos to all of us. And perhaps it is not too much to hope that this exhibition which we inaugurate today may stimulate a more systematic effort to save the remainder of his work from the constant danger of destruction.

However that may be, this exhibition is an important moment in the history of modern Greek painting. And I mean "painting" — without an epithet; not just "popular" painting.

Theophilos was indeed a man of the people. In the eyes of the world he was a lunatic. He could be heard to say the strangest things about his art; he could be seen rushing about the streets dressed up as Alexander the Great and escorted by a flock of street urchins dressed up as "Macedonians."* People made fun of him, sometimes very roughly; once they shook the ladder on which he was working and made him fall down. Such are the inconveniences of having to deal with those who are unlike ourselves. But this peripatetic painter gave his all, like a true artist, to his creation. And this creation is an important event in Greek painting. I do not mean an event that illustrates what might be described as the folklore side of art, as we might be induced to think by looking at the local costumes, the fustanellas, the milkmaids on the hillsides, the various faces of the popular heroes whom he reproduces, or by concentrating on his superficial technical weaknesses, his lack of "school," his "primitiveness," as it might be called. It is an event that gives a lesson in painting itself, that gives aid and illumination to those who are able and willing to use their eyes, even to those

* Here a carnival costume representing ancient Greek warriors.

who come from the most famous studios of Western Europe. After Theophilos we no longer see things in the same way. This is what is important, and this is something that we were not told by all those distinguished professors of the great academies.

Theophilos gave us a new eye. He cleansed our seeing — just as after a brief shower we see the skies shining, and the houses, the red soil, and the tiniest leaves on the bushes. He has something about him that is like the trembling of the dew. Maybe he is not a virtuoso; maybe in this sphere his ignorance of technique is great. But he has this enormously rare thing, this thing that before him was impossible to achieve with a Greek landscape: a moment of color and of air, held there in all its inner life and the radiation of its movement; this poetic rhythm (what other words can I use?) which makes the impossible connection, binding together what is scattered, restoring what is corruptible; this human breath that was there in the sturdy tree, in the hidden flower or in the dancing movement of a dress — all this we have missed so much, because so much we have longed to see it. And this was the grace given to us by Theophilos. And this is not folklore.

I am conscious that I am speaking awkwardly, that this emotion of mine may be considered just a lack of critical judgment. Still, it is an emotion that I have been trying to control for thirteen years, ever since the time when, with infinite reverence, my good friend the poet Andreas Embiricos first showed me the paintings of Theophilos. Since then, every time I have seen these pictures again it has been as though I were seeing them for the first time. It was as though the walls of a parlor came crashing down, the walls of the enormously depressing painting that has been done so often and has been so easy to do in the years since the rebirth of Greek independence. I felt the same emotion when I first read the *Memoirs* of Makryannis.

I have not the least wish to exalt the uneducated at the expense of the educated, or to suggest that there is anything harmful in disciplined training and in knowledge. Like many friends of our painter who are much more competent and efficient in these things than I am, I believe just the opposite. Because education and knowledge are a training in life; and for a training in life one can learn much from people like Theophilos who have worked in the dark but found their way searching along the dark passages of what is, I believe a very cultivated collective soul — the soul of our people. There is indeed much to be gained here. What we have to beware of is half-education — the little learning that ends up by both distorting the mind and putting it to sleep. And from this point of view I should find it very hard to admit that Theophilos was uneducated. He is not even an unusual phenomenon. The odd formation and special shape of the Greek way of expression must lead us, I think, to some such conclusions as these. For example a popular song passed on from mouth to mouth, "among the parlormaids" as they used to say, becomes the *Erotocritos*, the cornerstone of the creative work of Solomos, who was one of the most cultivated men in Europe. And the two foremost monuments of Greek prose are *The Woman of Zante* by this same master of culture and the *Memoirs* of Makryannis, who could scarcely read. And in painting there sometimes appears a genius like Theotocopoulos, who could defend his methods before the Grand Inquisition, and sometimes a Theophilos, an outlandish figure in his antiquated costume, who goes round the villages of Pelion with paintbrushes stuck in his waistband and is described by the village women as a lunatic and a loafer.

Greek cultural heritage is so vast that no one really knows who is going to be called to carry out its designs in practice. There are times when this heritage is in the hands of the most famous men in the history of the world, and there are other times when it goes into hiding among the nameless, waiting for the reappearance of the great names. Anyone who takes the trouble to look into this endless adventure will learn a lesson of great value. Our folk song can, in the sensitivity of one and the same person, throw fresh light on Homer and fill in the meaning of Aeschylus. This is no small thing, and it is a thing that could only happen in Greece.

After this clarification, we may look in a somewhat more relaxed way at this man of the people — Theophilos. This is not the time to tell the story of his life, but I would not like to end without mentioning what was perhaps the most valuable thing among his possessions — the little chest in which he kept the tools of his trade and his books. It is a small wooden chest, completely covered with his own paintings — Iphigenia in Aulis, heroes of the War of Independence like Diakos, Botzaris, Grivas — and it is all decorated with the strange and startling flowers of this gardener of eager manhood and of love. The friend who saved it keeps it as it was found by the side of the dead painter on the eve of the feast of the Annunciation in 1934. Open it, and you will find yourself (it is a shattering experience) gazing at the footprints of the life of a great man. By "great" I mean "whole." One feels the presence of that very rare thing — a being who never once wasted anything at all. From the commonest and most ephemeral articles — things manufactured to stay with us only for a very short time, things made only to amuse the pathos of a life that wishes for nothing except to forget itself — the life of simple people or of children; paper flowers tossed by the wind in the narrow streets of some provincial town at carnival time or at Easter or at a local merrymaking — the things are there to show from what small origins springs the force of the fascination of a master. His books: penny leaflets or school texts, worn out, about the lives of the Ancients, lives of saints, the *Octoechos*, *Erotocritos*, the story of Puss in Boots, of Little Red Riding Hood, ballads of war and of love. And next to his books his gallery: postcards, cheap chromos, collected when he was a door guard at the Greek Consulate in Smyrna; manly heroes; beautiful women like the ones we used to see on the hand organs; sea battles of the Russo-Japanese War; receptions of the Great Mogul; couples of the old sentimental times; and among all these his notebook, a big copybook of cheap paper, in which he copies out from books and newspapers landscapes and scenes of ancient times, statues of the gods, battles of Alexander the Great and innumerable busts of heroes, ancient and contemporary.

These were the museums and galleries to which Theophilos went and from them he tried to learn what he did learn. There is no denying it: Theophilos did sometimes get his start from these small things. But it would be a great mistake to believe that in this industry of his lies the essence of his painting. Let any creator who did not start from small things cast the first stone. I remember the lines of Yeats:

> Those masterful images, because complete,
> Grew in pure mind, but out of what began?
> A mound of refuse or the sweepings of a street. . . .

One of our best young painters told me what he felt when he first saw the paintings of Theophilos: "But this man is asking a lot — too much: He is asking for the whole truth." And the truth — the whole truth — that Theophilos gives us is his own world that is wholly alive, a pictorial world without tricks and subterfuges, where things do not fall to the ground as real loaves do. This extraordinary power that he has can transform, according to his own rhythm, everything that he touches. Possessed by the passion for expression, he absorbs and creates his painting wherever he can and wherever he finds it. So he goes on painting till the end of his life, on every surface that he can lay his hands on — wood, cloth, tins, rags, walls of houses or shops. This much was given him by God, and this small man used the gift of God for creation, this small man, this visionary, as I see him in one of his old photographs. Theophilos sometimes took his figures from photos, lithographs, or postcards. He did so and perhaps it was an empirical way of sometimes giving his intellect a rest and of liberating the "demon" inside him. Vincenzos Cornaros* took the figures of his poem from a French romance of chivalry — a sort of chromo of his time. Such things often happen. But what does not often happen is an *Erotocritos*, or the light of Theophilos, which remains there as it was on the first day of the creation of the world.

* Cretan poet of the seventeenth century; author of the long love epic *Erotocritos*.

II

Sikelianos

THE death of the poet is the consummation of a birth. Angelos Sikelianos has passed away. Now his work, outside the shadow of this great man, rises up in its entirety, finding its realization in a light that is absolute,

> Like an almond tree dressed only in its blossoms without a single leaf,
> A white mass of flower going down to the depths of the mind, a silence all of flowers.

And so, as we measure the depth of the chasm left by the passing of Angelos Sikelianos, what I think of is this flowering silence of a birth. It is difficult to explain when one's emotion so presses upon one. Nevertheless, just as I try my best to grasp and keep his living human presence among us, I think again that it was he himself who put all the fervor of his soul into an effort to embrace life and death together. I can think of no other figure who awakes in the mind so many images of burial and of resurrection. Indeed, I would say that his work could be set in the frame of that loftiest form of springtime that I know — a Greek Passion Week.

Broadcast from the BBC (London, July 7, 1951).

ON THE GREEK STYLE

As the years go by, and with the help of our poets, we, listening to the echoes of our tradition, begin to understand from what depths they proceed; gradually we sort out the qualities that distinguish us from the world around us. We see, sometimes, that our feelings when real, the symbols of our creed when the faith is real, and our instinctiveness because it has traveled into so many generations so far into time, and has roots not only among us but also far away — all these have a harmonious and extended wealth and a kind of tone that is sometimes extremely singular. How singular it can be can be seen by considering the great poets we have had in the last hundred and fifty years. If one imagines them as the cardinal points marking the horizon of an idea, the Greek idea, and if one tries to observe how peculiarly different they are from each other and at the same time how strikingly similar, one will perhaps have some notion of the extent and the pattern of our spiritual territory. We shall see something that is always true to itself, yet still mysterious, still antithetical, as are all things which pulsate with life.

Our tradition is full of contrasts. Only great men can bring them into harmony. In Greece there are the figures of Dionysus and of the Crucified Lord. But it needed the powerful pressure of the voice of Sikelianos to incarnate this word in our flesh:

> Sweet child of mine, my Dionysus and my Christ.

It is in this way that I think of the image of the Mother of God, who is so close to him. And I think of dreams such as the following, which must have taken its color from the iconostasis of his childhood:

> . . . I saw my father stretched out beside me,
> pushing aside his winding sheet
> to spring up stark naked before my eyes,
> in greater beauty, greater maturity,
> his flesh like rosebuds
> full of light,
> and say to me,
> "My son, I have won freedom!"

And I try to survey the religious feeling of Sikelianos from its beginnings in his ancestral Christianity in Levkas, nurtured there by every breath from the soil of Greece, extending and assimilating myths which we were sure had been long dead, moving through Dionysus and Hades, who are one and the same, as Heraclitus has it, and always seeking for a resurrection, a rebirth: "High Greece."

In the years when Sikelianos was an adolescent, the whole of our intellectual world was quickened by the spur of this yearning.

> In the mind of Greek youth
> bathed in the new,
> the rosy light deep down
> is staged the drama
> of the struggle of the young god,
> the young Apollo
> when he killed the Dragon.

ON THE GREEK STYLE

This is the era of Palamas, but among the many expressions of this era I would refer only to the picture Sikelianos himself gives us of Pericles Yannopoulos.* He and Sikelianos are as alike as brothers.

> And the love of the beautiful body and of the sun,
> of the rhythmical strength which declares
> beauty effortlessly,
> with only a movement, with only
> a quick smile, with only
> a quick and limpid laughter
> like a raven's cry in the abyss
> of the sheen of these Attic skies
> clean and unsponsored reborn to life
> in his smile and in his movements.
> O Attica! and no one breathed
> that delicate fragrance of yours
> with so lordly a feeling, no one so took
> your unexpected colors
> to hold within tight-pressed eyelids,
> and take into his flesh your frugal spirit.
> We know no one among us
> so like your olive tree,
> the blond ear of corn and again
> your golden yellow marbles.

But Sikelianos was a much more powerful creator than Yannopoulos. He too felt that passionate and burning flame which devoured Yannopoulos and directed him to ride on horseback to his tomb beneath the sea, but he was also able, with the force

* Pericles Yannopoulos. Prose writer (1869–1910). He committed suicide by riding on horseback into the sea of Salamis, near Eleusis.

of Dionysus running pure in his veins, to raise up a present, a contemporary life from the farthest and the most impenetrable sanctuaries of our tradition. At the sound of his voice a whole forgotten world rises from the tomb, like a Day of Judgment rooted in a Greek landscape, breathing with all the morning dew of the primeval vision, rooted in the senses of man. Sikelianos sees things without a break and with no refraction. And just as he refuses to separate death from the most fervent moment of life, just as he refuses to separate his own body from the body of his country, so he struggles to unite the world of the gods with the world of men. In Sikelianos there is an anthropism that is Hellenic and that is holy:

> . . . and we say that it is possible for earth
> to mingle with the stars, like a deep plow with a plowfield,
> and for the sky to nurse the ears of wheat. O Father,
> at times our hearts are burdened down and loaded
> with the bitterness of life and all its weight.

But I did not mean to go on talking about the poetry of Sikelianos. All I wanted to do was to remain a little longer with the friend whom we have lost.

I met him late in my life, and I feel that this was my own fault. What I think of as our first real meeting was after I first read the manuscript of "The Sacred Way."

> I felt the sun was pouring down into my heart
> through the new wound that fate had opened in me,

so strong a setting, as when after a sudden split of
   timbers
the waves rush in to the ship and force it down.

I remember gratefully the freshness of the emotion aroused in me by this tone of a strength somehow wounded, yet ripe and mature. Later, whenever I saw him in the country or heard the villagers speak of his walks over their fields, I always used to think of him with that monastic walking stick of his, a gift from Faneromeni, which was to help his steps, as he used to say, along this road of the soul, as he called the Sacred Way, which was also the last road taken by Yannopoulos. I liked to admire this lord of our language in the setting of our Greek landscape, a landscape which he enjoyed so intimately and which he touched with his own presence — marbles, hills, shores — just as a shepherd touches the familiar furniture of his hut. I liked the way the simple people of the hills and plains called him Kyr Angelos. I was moved by this life of his which had achieved so rare a thing — a cleanliness and a purity in things both great and small.

So I felt about him too in the last years, whenever I was given the chance to see him in his long agony. Because the fate of this man, who said at the very beginning "The only method is death," was that he should live long on the threshold of the underworld. He lived through this period as he lived at all times, with the same noble-minded enjoyment, with the same air and grace with which he knew how to choose and give away a rose. I remember him one night in his house; he had been struck by a heavy blow which seemed the last deferred one upon this wounded lion. "I saw," he told me, "the absolute blackness. It was ineffably beautiful." I was starting on a long journey. I did not know whether I would see him again. I felt the wings of a great angel beating in the room. It was as if we were touched by the breath of things we had never seen, and yet we love them more than anything else in life — the air, the style of a Greece that all of us seek so passionately and which is attained by so very few.

On my way out I found myself whispering the last strophe of "The Great Homecoming":

> Because I know it: in depths beyond the clustered
>   light of stars,
> hidden and like an eagle
> there waits for me, where the divine darkness begins,
> the self-same, my first self.

I was looking at the resurrection of the stars.

III

Makryannis

THE name of Makryannis for most Athenians means merely a section of the town, just off the Acropolis; some scholars and specialists in the history of Greece between the years 1820 and 1850 will recall the actions of the man — General Makryannis, hero of the War of Independence, leader of the popular insurrection that gave the nation the Constitution of 1843, inmate of the prison of the first King Otho and his Bavarian court. But only a few people are aware that Makryannis — perhaps because he was wholly unlettered — has given us a document of great significance, the story of his life.

The Makryannis of the *Memoirs* was first noticed with respect by a handful of young people who began to write just after the catastrophe for Greece in Asia Minor that followed upon the end of the First World War. I do not think I shall be far from the mark if I say that between 1925 and 1935 the voice of Makryannis was being introduced timidly and almost in a whisper into the Greek literary world. This was not a fact that could be known to the public at large. These young people, who grew up during the First World War and were in the prime

---

A lecture given twice in Egypt — Alexandria, May 16, 1943, and Cairo, May 19, 1963.

of life at the beginning of the new conflagration, did not have the time either for their own work to come to maturity or to see established the new set of values for which they were looking. However, anyone who cares to follow closely the various patterns of Greek intellectual life which appeared during the years between the wars will recognize that directly after the disaster in Asia Minor there was a deep change in the way Greeks thought; it was a period of accounts — the closing of some, the opening of others — comparable to the period of transformation which followed the war of 1897. This intellectual struggle has been submerged — or perhaps has been intensified — by the Second World War. And this is why Makryannis, who had already found the way to the hearts of the young, will have to wait for the all-clear signal before he can take the place which he deserves.

I feel — and I hope my audience feels this too — that while in the present circumstances it is difficult for me, in the limited span of a short lecture, to persuade you of the importance of this book of Makryannis's, at least I can point out to you the path I followed myself in my approach to a work so generally ignored. So I must ask you to give an unprejudiced attention to the few passages which I shall quote — and I must beg you for your good will.

However, I have something here to gladden my heart, now that I am attempting to record what

MAKRYANNIS

I think about this most unusual text. You, who have shown your interest by coming to listen to me tonight, have given me the opportunity to try to settle a debt of gratitude that has been weighing on my conscience for many years. Since 1926, when I first held in my hands *The Memoirs of General Makryannis* down to this very day, no month has passed without my reading some of its pages, no week without my thinking of some of the exquisitely vital passages which I have found there. These pages have been my companions through voyages and peregrinations; in joys and sorrows they have been sources of illumination and of consolation. In this country of ours, where we are sometimes so cruelly self-taught, Makryannis has been the humblest and also the steadiest of my teachers.

I always believed that I would be given the opportunity to show him some small token of my gratitude. It is a strange coincidence that this opportunity should be given here and now, in the Greek camp of the Middle East, among the Greeks of Egypt. And now at this moment [1943], when our eyes and thoughts are fixed on the fate of Hellenism and we are trying to follow it from the middle of the tempest and beyond the sharp corner taken by world history in our times, there may be — who knows? — some hidden meaning in this coincidence. These are times when the struggle, the blood, the pain and the thirst for justice strip away from the soul the temporary comforts of narcotics and illusions, when what man asks from his fellow man is something that is clean, strong, and sympathetic. In such times it is good to speak of men like Makryannis. Listen to him:

"What I write down I write down because I cannot bear to see the right stifled by the wrong. For this reason I learned to write in my old age and to do this crude writing, because I did not have the means to study when I was a child. I was poor and I went into service and looked after the horses and did all sorts of jobs so that I could pay my father's debt to the tax people and so that I myself could live in this society so long as I have my God's pledge in my body.* And since God willed that my country should rise from the dead and be freed from the tyranny of the Turks, he made me also able to contribute to the best of my ability — less than the worst of the Greeks. Many wise men write books and learned editors and foreigners write about Greece. It was just one thing that made me write too: it is that this country of ours belongs to all of us, learned and ignorant, rich and poor, politicians and soldiers, even the least of the people. All of us who fought the war, each man as he could, must live here now. The reason why we all fought was that we might keep this country for all of us together, so that neither the strong nor the weak should say 'I.' Do you know when one can say 'I'?

* The soul.

When a man struggles all by himself and all by himself makes or breaks something, then he may say 'I.' But when many people join together in the struggle and accomplish something then they should say 'We.' In the life which we live it is 'We' and not 'I.' And from now on let us learn wisdom if we want to be able to live together. I wrote the naked truth so that all Greeks should see that the struggle is for their country and their faith; so that my children may see this and say 'This is what we have, our fathers' struggles, our fathers' sacrifices' — if they are indeed struggles and sacrifices; so that they may follow the example and work for the good of their country, their faith and their society, that they become better themselves. Not that they should be conceited about the deeds of their fathers, that they should prostitute virtue and trample down the law and mistake influence for ability."

So he ends his manuscript, a manuscript which, in book form, extends to more than 460 large closely printed pages. Makryannis begins it on the 26th of February 1829, when he is about thirty-two years old, in the town of Argos, where we find him as "Chief of the Executive Power of Peloponnesus and Sparta." Writing in the form of a diary, he notes the events of the day and also recalls events that happened earlier. He goes on with his book in Nauplia and in Athens until 1840, when he closes it in a hurry in order to hide it. He is a suspect to the authorities. "They had great suspicion of me," he writes, "and wanted to search my house to find my writings." So he entrusts the manuscript to a relation, who takes it to the island of Tinos. In 1844 — that is, after the successful rising of the constitutionalists, among whom he played a great part himself, and after the events of the September Revolution [1843], he goes to Tinos and fetches his manuscript back. He copies into it the notes that he has been keeping in the meantime and with infinite precaution. "I wrote my notes," he says, "and had a tin can into which I shoved them." He continues writing until April 1850, and after about a year he puts the finishing touches to his book by adding a prologue and a fairly long epilogue. The masterly edition of this manuscript by the great scholar Yanis Vlahoyannis — still the only one that exists — was first published in 1907, which means that for half a century this invaluable text was unavailable, lost in absolute darkness.

Makryannis was an illiterate. Although he reached the rank of general he came from humble origins. His father was a poor shepherd of Roumelia on the Greek mainland. This is how he reports his own birth: "My birthplace is off Lidoriki, a village in the district of Lidorikion called Avoriti. My parents were very poor and their poverty was caused by the rapacity of the Turks and of the Albanians of Ali Pasha. They were poor and had a large family, and when I was still in my mother's womb, she went one day to gather firewood in the forest.

With the wood on her back, burdened and in the absolute wilderness, the pains came upon her and she gave birth to me. Alone and tired, she risked her life and mine. After the birth, she tidied herself, took up the burden of firewood, put some green leaves on top, laid me on the leaves and went back to the village."

As he says, he did not have the means to go to a teacher. He was just capable of writing, and it is doubtful if he could actually read anything except what he wrote himself. "Brave Makryannis, unread forever," was said of him by Alexander Soutzos* in the days of the September Revolution of 1843. After all, his handwriting is a purely personal invention. "Coarse writing," he calls it himself. It took Vlahoyannis seventeen months' work to read, or rather to decipher it and to produce an intelligible copy. And a glance at a single page of this huge manuscript will soon show one why. Phonetic transcriptions of local Roumelia speech, bizarre improvised couplings of letters make the page look like an endless succession of spidery arabesques. There are no signs to mark a paragraph or any other interruption; there is not even any punctuation. Only occasionally does a kind of perpendicular bar mark a major stop. The text looks like an old wall in which, if one looks closely, one can trace every movement of the builder, how he fitted one stone

---

* Poet (1803–1863). He wrote lyrical, political and satirical verse. He was very much involved in the political events of the time.

to the next, how he adjusted every effort he made to what had gone before and was to follow after, leaving on the finished building the imprint of the adventures of an uninterrupted human action. This is the thing that so moves us and to which we give the name of style or rhythm. So in this handwriting of Makryannis, illegible as it may appear to the ordinary reader, we can discern even more clearly than from the words themselves the abiding will of the author to paint his own very self upon the paper.

When he was in Argos, Makryannis, in order that he should not "run to the taverns," used to ask his various friends to help add a little to his education — and his knowledge was well below the standards even of a period that was not remarkable for its literacy. He often feels very humble because of his lack of learning: "I ought not to set out on this task, I, an illiterate, to be a burden to the honorable readers and the great men and the wise in this society." He insists again and again: "I am an illiterate, and do not know how to keep order in my writings." He asks forgiveness for indulging "as a human being" in this "weakness." Such matters should be written about "by learned men and not by simple illiterates." And the others, the learned men, adopt a rather condescending attitude towards him. "I cannot wield the sword, and he cannot wield the pen," says Soutzos again, and characteristically; "therefore it is best for each of us to stick to what he does best." But Makryannis writes of the fatherland which "has been despoiled, dishonored and is going all wrong because we have all been found to be wild beasts," men of religion, politicians, military leaders alike. And it is "a general country, a country for each one of us." It is for this reason that the truth should be spoken out loud by both the learned and the simple.

Obviously Makryannis would like to have had the means to become educated. But this fact does not make him a lesser man, does not, as we say, give him an inferiority complex. He feels, and makes us feel with him, that he is a man on whom God has conferred the gift of speech, a gift which no one has the right to take away from him. Wherever he may be, whether in a palace or in a cottage, he speaks his mind and he speaks with confidence. And because he has this innate confidence in his power of expression, he can speak with color, with a wide spectrum of varying shades, with tonality and with rhythm. I have the impression that any philologist who wants to criticize this difficult transcription of Makryannis's text should be careful first of all to base his work on his own ability to hear the spoken word.

Makryannis respects knowledge. "He fought like a lion, and he led us like a philosopher" is what he says of Gogos, the first leader under whom he served in war. But this certainly does not prevent him from expressing his feelings about pedantry or the peddling around of ancestors.

"You put a new leader in the fortress of Corinth," he says to the politicians of the period, "and his name was Achilles. And hearing the name of Achilles, you imagined that this was the great Achilles, and you let the name fight the Turks. But fighting is not done by a name; what does the fighting is gallantry, patriotism, courage. And your Achilles of Corinth was a fine figure. Yes, he was called Achilles. And he had in the fortress everything necessary for fighting, and he had a great army. He saw in the distance the Turks of Dramali (and they were already feeling the strain of the battles in Roumelia and Dervenia), and at the very first sight Achilles left the fort and fled without striking a blow. Now if Nikitas had been there, would he have done that? Would Hajdichristo and the rest have done that? Of course not. Because they fought Dramali in the plain and routed him — in the plain and not from a well-stocked fort like that of Corinth."

Learning is one of the noblest exercises of man and to be learned is one of his highest desires. Education is the governing factor of life. And since these first principles are true, we must not forget that there is a good education — the one that liberates man and helps him to live according to his true nature — and a bad education — the one that distorts and desiccates and is a kind of industry for producing half-baked intellectuals, the nouveaux riches of learning, who have exactly the same bogus good breeding as their counterparts in society. And I fear that if Makryannis had received a formal education at that period, he would have had to deny his real self, since education in those days was in the hands of those whom Palamas calls "trophy-bearers of the empty word," and who are still far from being extinct. I do not congratulate Makryannis on his illiteracy, but I give thanks to the good God that he did not have the means to become educated. Because if he had gone to a teacher, we should perhaps have a book many times the size of the *Memoirs*, a book full of bell-ringing and exhibitionism; we should have much more information about the history of the period; we should have perhaps another Soutzos, writing in prose; but what we should not have is that untarnished spring of life which is the book that Makryannis did write. And that would be a great loss. Because we see, as Makryannis comes closer to us, that though he was illiterate, he was very far from being an uncultured barbarian from the hills. He was exactly the opposite: he was one of the most cultivated souls in the Greek world. And the culture, the education, which Makryannis shows is not fragmentary, is not, as it were, a piece of private property. It is the common lot, the spiritual wealth of a race, handed on through the ages from millennium to millennium, from generation to generation, from the sensitive to the sensitive; persecuted and always alive, ignored and always present — the common lot of Greek popular tradition. It is the essence, precisely, of this civilization, this differentiated energy that formed the men and the nation that in 1821 decided to live in freedom or to die.

This is why our popular tradition is so important.

Once upon a time there was a poor kilted man who had a mania for painting. His name was Theophilos. He used to carry his paintbrushes in his belt, where our ancestors used to carry their pistols and swords. He used to go round the villages of Mytilene and the villages of Mount Pelion painting. He painted whatever he was asked to paint, for this was how he got his bread. In Ano-Volos there are whole rooms painted by the hand of Theophilos, there are coffee shops in Lesbos, groceries and shops in various places marking his trail — if, that is, they are still preserved. People used to make fun of him. They teased him brutally. Theophilos, however, never stopped painting. I have seen his "canvases," made of cardboard or cheap sailcloth. A group of young writers showed respect for them and were considered to be unbalanced by the academicians. So time went by and Theophilos died, not so many years ago. Then a traveler came here from Paris. He saw the paintings, took some fifty examples, packed them up and showed them to the illustrious critics of the Seine. And the illustrious critics gave this verdict: "Theophilos is a great painter," and we in Athens could hear our jaws drop.

The moral of this story is that popular education is concerned not only with how we should teach the people but with how we should learn from the people.

I always remember Theophilos when I think of Makryannis. I was saying that Makryannis is one of the most cultivated souls of the Greek world, and I should say the same thing of Theophilos, if the word "culture" carries the meaning of spiritual form. And this culture of theirs is extremely intense and active. It is the extraordinary necessity which they feel to express themselves. It is something that overrides all difficulties. One thinks of those obstinate plants which, once they have taken root, will grow on and on, demolishing hedges, breaking up tombstones.

Makryannis never stops working at the means of expression. He will even use pebbles from the sea to represent in his little garden an idea that comes into his head; he will complete the thought of the day by the dreams he has in his sleep.

Once he goes on a trip to Acarnania. He sees and "points down" the places where the battles of the Revolution were fought. On his return to Athens he decides to have some paintings made of the battles of the wars of liberation.

"I took," he tells us, "a Frankish [foreign] painter and had him paint these battles. I did not speak his language. He did two or three; they were no good. I paid him and he left. When I had dismissed this painter I sent for a war veteran from Sparta, Panayotis Zographos by name . . . and I sent for his two children and had them in my house when they worked. This started in 1836 and ended in 1839. I used to take the painter and go with him to the hills and tell him, 'The place was like this or like that; this battle was fought like this; this was the chief of the Turks and this was the chief of the Greeks.' "

In this way twenty-five paintings were completed. They would have been totally lost but for their chance discovery by Ioannis Gennadios.*

These paintings, done by the hand of Panayotis Zographos and by the inspiration of Makryannis, are among the rarest and the most vital monuments of popular art which we possess. They are of the kind which suddenly reveal to us areas of splendor in the soul of our people.

These paintings illustrate in meticulous detail the battles with which they deal, almost like a plan of campaign or military document, and are at the same time a joy to the eye. I once saw a man burst into tears as he looked at them for the first time. Sometimes they remind you of popular needlework — like that brilliant picture of the siege of Athens.

* Envoy to London 1885–1892 and a well-known book collector. One set of the twenty-five paintings of Zographos is in the Gennadion Library, Athens. Another is in the Royal Library, Windsor Castle, England.

Sometimes they bring you back to gardens which have remained green and fresh since the artist first saw them. Sometimes they make you breathe that atmosphere of enchantment and fear which is found in a fairy story. It is a rhapsody that is old and at the same time we are hearing it for the first time.

There was an occasion when Colettis, the Greek Ambassador in Paris, sent to Makryannis a visitor with a letter of introduction — the Marquis Raoul de Malherbe. "He also wanted some Greek songs," Makryannis notes, "so I made five or six for him." Makryannis is like the unknown poets of our popular songs; he "makes" a song; and what a revelation it is when he allows us to see how this despised sensibility of the people feels and loves the works of ancient art!

"I had two statues," he writes, "wonderful ones, a woman and a king's son, all of one piece and their veins showing, so perfect they were. When Poros was sacked they were taken by some soldiers and they would have sold them to some Europeans in Argos; they were asking a thousand talers. . . . I took those soldiers aside and told them this: You must not give away these things, not even for ten thousand talers; you must not let them leave the country; it was for them we fought."

You see? It is not Lord Byron speaking, nor a great scholar nor an archaeologist. It is a shepherd's son from Roumelia, his body covered with wounds. "It was for them we fought." There is more weight in this sentence of a simple man than in the effusions of fifteen gilded academies. Because it is only in feelings like this that the culture of a nation can be rooted — in real feelings, and not in abstractions about the beauty of our famous ancestors or in hearts that have become dried up from a cataleptic fear of the common people.

"From the bones of our slain," writes Solomos,* and the idea he expresses is a true one. It was from the bones of Greeks, the dead and the living, that the Greek Revolution arose. And this is why, against all possible odds, it succeeded; this is why it never stopped throughout the nineteenth century and is still going on today. It is no overstatement to say that the war in which our country is engaged today is a continuation of the Revolution of 1821. We should remember this: it is only when our race goes back to the people, seeks illumination from the spirit of the people, and is reshaped by the people that we are following in the tradition that came into our national consciousness through the Greek Revolution. That struggle was a social, political, and military event. It was also an intellectual event. This aspect of the Revolution (a most neglected aspect) is very significantly illustrated by the testimony of Makryannis. Historical events do not come to an end so as to fit in with the date charts that we find in history books.

* The first and greatest poet of modern Greece. Born in Zante in 1798. Died in Corfu in 1857.

2

THE life of Makryannis covers a considerable portion of the history of Hellenism during the first sixty years of the last century. He was born in 1797 and died on April 27, 1864. It is impossible to tell the whole story of his life. All I shall do is to quote some more passages from his *Memoirs,* in which he shows us how he sees events and how he reacts to them. The story of Makryannis is more than a history of events. It is the story of how the people felt towards the events of that great period in which the Greece of today was born.

Makryannis was still a baby when his family, persecuted by the local Turks and Albanians ("they wanted to enslave the village"), was forced to take refuge in the town of Levadia. At the age of seven he went out to work as a domestic servant to help his family. "They wanted me to do all the lowest and most menial jobs in the house," he says, "and this was death to me." He went out of his way to make himself insupportable and was dismissed. At the age of fourteen we find him with a fellow villager at Desphina. He relates the following incident: "I was about fourteen when I went to a fellow countryman in Desphina. . . . It was the feast of St. John and there was a great gathering of people for the feast. We went there. He gave me his gun to hold. I wanted to have a shot with it. The gun broke. He then gave me a terrible beating in front of everybody. I did not mind the beating; what I minded was this humiliation in front of the people. Then everyone was eating and drinking and I was crying. I could not find anyone to whom I could tell my grievances. It seemed to me that the right thing would be to go to St. John, since it was in his house that I had been injured and insulted. I went to his church at night and shut the door and started crying and lamenting and bowing down to him. 'Why did he do this to me? Am I a beast of burden that I should be beaten like that?' And I begged the saint to give me some fine arms covered in silver and fifteen purses of silver; then I would make him a fine silver chandelier. After a lot of talking the saint and I came to an understanding."

Came to an understanding with the saint . . . And as a matter of fact the Christian saint kept his promises much better than Apollo used to do. Makryannis now goes to Arta and works under a Thanassi Lidorikis. Later he works on his own and does well, becoming quite prosperous, so that on the eve of the Revolution he had "the affluence of God." "Then," he says, "I had made for me a silver gun and silver pistols and arms and a good silver chandelier. Carrying my arms and wearing good clothes, I took the chandelier and brought it to my patron and my true friend St. John, and it stands there in his church to this day. And I bowed to him with tears from my innermost heart, as I remembered all the humiliations I had suffered."

In 1820 he joined the secret society of the Philiké Hetairia, the organization which prepared the way for the Revolution. "I entered the secret," he says, "and went to my house and did the work I did loyally for God and for my country, so that she should not call me a thief or a brigand, but that she should call me her own son and I should call her my mother."

We find him at Patras when the first shots are fired. He is there ostensibly "as a merchant," but his real assignment is to collect information and maintain contact with the revolutionary leaders. When back in Arta, he is captured and condemned to be hanged. He escapes and has his first fighting under Gogos Bacolas. He fights at Peta, at the siege and the storming of Arta. There followed the exodus from the town and the flight of the non-combatants. In all this disorder, as he sees men plundering and looting, his reaction is immediate: "Since then," he says, "seeing this kind of virtue, I was disgusted with us Greeks. We were just cannibals." This humanity of his will bring him later, in Athens, into violent opposition to Odysseus and Gouras.

So his military record begins. From April 1822, when we find him as chief of four villages near Salona in eastern Greece, until the battle of Piraeus in April 1827, when he is fighting with "practically my whole body covered with bandages," Makryannis fights without stopping. The details of these campaigns will be found in the excellent volume of Vlahoyannis. Here I should like to confine myself to his description of the battle of October 7, 1826, around the besieged Acropolis. In this battle Makryannis had the task of defending what is now the theater of Herodes Atticus. It is described as "the most serious of all the battles fought for the Acropolis."

"I was sleepless night after night. We worked day and night. . . . I fell asleep. The Turks, hearing the blows of Lagoumidji, get together and charge. Then my men engaged the Turks. I got up quickly from the place where I was lying. I rushed to the rampart. The Turks shot at me. I started shooting at them too, right into the middle of them. In one burst of firing they wounded me in the neck. Then I tried to stand on my feet and to come down from the rampart. I fell down. The place was very narrow. The men were crowded together outside. They were forced back from the outer rampart. They trampled on me to get past. The place was narrow and they nearly finished me. They saw the blood and imagined I was dead. Most of them came past, there were only a few more and they also tried to get into the fortification, and then the Turks would have got in with them. . . . Then I stood up and with my sword I made about ten men stay where they were. I would not let them inside. And I shut the door that was left open and we started to fight with our pistols. Neither the Turks nor we could use our guns. . . . The Turks charged again. They wounded me again in the head, right at the top of it. My body was drenched in blood. My men tried to make me go inside. Then I said to them, 'Brothers, whether we go in or stay out, we are done for unless we keep the Turks back.' Then the noble Greeks held their ground like lions. . . . At dusk I issued new ammunition. More of our comrades came to reinforce us. New troops also reinforced the Turks. They charged again, got inside the arcades and occupied all of them. They made a breach in the wall and began to fire right into the fort. They came on in a rush to seize our sector of the rampart. There they killed Dalamangas and five or six others. I was hit by another bullet, very badly this time, at the back of the head. The material of my headdress was forced through the bones, right up to the outer shroud of the brain. I fell down, as good as dead. My men started to drag me inside. Then I came back to my senses. I said, 'Let me die where I am, so that I may never live to see the Turks holding my post.' Then the poor Greeks had pity on me. They fought gallantly. They drove the Turks down from our rampart, and back to the arcades."

With the coming of Capo d'Istria and of Otho began the tragic misunderstandings between those who made the Revolution and those who were to govern the country for the next thirty-five years. It was a long drama played out between abstract ideas and the life that had sprung up as a force to liberate a small and tortured nation, a life that was, if you like, undisciplined but was also strong, efficient, sensitive and suffering — even more sensitive and even more prone to suffering since the wounds inflicted in the recent appalling struggle were still open; and in popular speech a wound that hurts is called "angry."

The people who undertook the task of governing this land were faced with a particularly difficult problem: how to bring order out of what they considered chaos; how to nurse, help and consolidate a nation that had just undergone a terrible ordeal in its struggle for freedom. What did these people do? They chose arbitrarily the easiest solution; with one stroke of the pen they effaced the problem altogether.

Let me explain. After the murder of Capo d'Istria, Greece experienced, in 1832, one of the worst years of her history. The country was divided into a number of military fiefs, each of which was concerned uniquely with feeding the hungry remnants of the armies of the Revolution. The new Bavarian Regency brought us a foreign loan. They could have used this money to provide a crust of bread for the starving veterans just outside the gates of Nauplia. Instead they preferred to employ these funds for the maintenance of the Bavarian army, which in their opinion would provide the support for the Regency and King Otho. With this foreign army they either disbanded the veterans or actually drove them out of Greece. These veterans were, they believed, just wild savages. And what did the savages think about it? We can see from this conversation which took place between Makryannis and Heydeck:

"Friend Heydeck was annoyed and answered me with much venom: 'You will do as you are told and no one will ask you for your opinion. Bavaria has thirty thousand bayonets and she will bring them here to crush you.' Then I felt in an awkward position. I said to him, 'Misery on us poor people! We shall go from bad to worse. I spoke to you as a friend and you answer me with bayonets. I tell you as a friend that you should try to make us love you and the King and not to be afraid of you. . . . If someone came and told me that it was necessary for the good of my country, I would willingly have both my eyes put out. Because if I am without eyes and my country prospers, she will feed me. But if my country is helpless, then I, even if I had ten eyes, would still be blind.' . . . He asks me, 'Do you not love the King?' 'No,' I tell him, 'I don't know how to tell lies. If my country is lost, then he cannot call me his subject and I cannot call him my King. And for this you should use justice and not threats with bayonets.' "

However, Makryannis was a man of good intentions. When Otho lands at Nauplia, he writes, "This day my country, so long lost and buried, has risen from the dead. . . . Our King has come who was given us through the power of God."

Certainly he never came into conflict with Otho personally. On the contrary, he tried to protect him from his evil councilors ("raw-hewn Bavarian duplicity" is the phrase he uses of them). For him the responsibility for the Regency is with Ludwig of Bavaria or with the foreign ambassadors, not with Otho himself.

"They took all the chiefs of the army and put them in prison and wanted to cut off their heads with the chopping instrument that these enlightened Europeans brought for us savage Greeks. But first England ought to cut off the head of her ambassador Dawkins, then France do the same for hers and Russia for hers, and then the Bavarian King should do the same for his three Regents and then he should chop off his own head. Because His Majesty is the gravedigger of our country and of our own innocent King."

But he is "no longer a boy"; he cannot bear to see "the wrong throttling the right"; he cannot bear to see the suffering of the veterans. In the following passage he is writing of the government of Capo d'Istria, but his feelings remain just the same:

"My country, you should praise and bless all the Greeks who sacrificed themselves for you, so that you should rise from the dead and be once more called a nation among nations, you, whose name had been crossed off the list of countries. You should praise and bless each and all of them. You should remember and honor those who first sacrificed themselves in Alamana, fighting against such a great force of Turks; and those who shut themselves in behind a fortification of bricks so weak as that of the Inn of Gravia; and those who crushed so many Turks and Pashas at Vasilika; and those who fought like lions at the Langada of Makrynoros, when they had to face simultaneous attacks at each of the two key passes, one at the Gate of Makrynoros and one at Thermopylae. And as the Turks advanced to force these passages, those immortals, those few, scarcely eighty-one of them at Langada, filled the place with bones. And they drove them back and routed them, these few, in the other pass, at Thermopylae, and elsewhere too. It was they who raised you from the dead and they let no army through, no supplies, no ammunition. It was they who put heart into the local bands who were besieging the Turks in their forts, and they starved them out and slaughtered them like goats. And at the end of it all, my country, it is these same people who are being persecuted by the Excellencies and the Eminences, by the Governor and by his brothers. The brothers of Capo d'Istria, Augustino and Biaro, are hunting down the wives and daughters of those men who died for us. It is these veterans whom they are now persecuting. They tell them to go and beg for their bread. 'Who told you,' they say, 'to bring misery on yourselves by taking up arms?' "

ON THE GREEK STYLE

These are the reasons which impel Makryannis to organize the conspiracy that ends with the granting of the Constitution of September 3, 1843. He makes everyone take an oath. This is how he does it. The scene is in Makryannis's house, at night; a veteran is sitting with him; they clink glasses and then the conversation proceeds:

" 'Where did you break that arm?' 'At Missolonghi,' he says. 'Where did I break mine?' 'At Myloi by Nauplia.' 'Why did we break them?' 'For the liberty of our country.' 'And where is liberty and justice now? Stand up!' And I go with him and make him take the oath."

And so the Constitution is achieved and it falls into the hands of politicians and is ridiculed. Makryannis becomes more and more isolated from the world.

"Those who today have our fate in their hands," he writes in about 1851, "those who govern us, big and small, ministers and members of parliament, regard it as an honor, a distinction, a sign of efficiency that it should be said of them that they have been thieves and traitors and have done so much harm to the country. They are the successful ones and they are rewarded for it. And those who are honest are persecuted and considered unworthy of society and the state."

Again: "You have shown your worth and what you have done for the country, all through from the beginning to the end. Inside and outside the country, people had their eyes on you and thought that you were something. And you are what you are. You were like the Sultan as the Europeans used to see him, and did not dare take away from him his title of 'Grand Seigneur.' As long as they saw his mosque in Vienna they were frightened of his coming nearer still and building more mosques. And because of their fear they sometimes even paid tribute to him. Then a handful of men appeared and showed that the Grand Seigneur has no more mosque-builders and that even the mosques he has now will come tumbling down. So from that time they have started calling him 'The Turk.' And because of this these benefactors of ours are enlightening us and making us progress. However, none of them has done us any real harm, and for that we should thank you, because you left us without weakness and made us what we are now."

Now only his old comrades come to visit him. But he is still suspect to the Government. Otho has never forgiven him for his part in the conspiracy of 1843. To the Government, Makryannis is the wild beast that has to be put in a cage. So, in September 1851, wild rumors begin to circulate — wild accusations that are never to be documented, never to be proved: Makryannis wants to assassinate the King, to proclaim the Republic; Makryannis is in touch with some Polish refugees who are distributing subversive literature; Makryannis made some disloyal statements to a certain A. Stephanides, a notorious blasphemer and the only witness to be called at the trial. So he is placed under house arrest. He is very ill. The seven wounds which he got in the wars are festering. "Often," said Dr. Goudas in his speech at Makryannis's funeral, "the wounds were open and bleeding. His body was wasted away by the ensuing fever. Serious complications set in from which his recovery was very slow. These were the rewards for his distinguished service to his country: wounds, pain, illness, and on top of it all a penury that was as incurable as these." The wounds in his head which he got during the battle of the Acropolis sometimes drive him out of his mind. Three days before he is taken to the Medresse jail — since, as in the days of his youth at the Church of St. John, he has no one else to whom he can appeal — he writes directly to God: "And you neither see us nor hear us. . . . And here I am bellowing night and day because of my wounds. And seeing my wretched family and my children drowned in tears and barefooted. And me being six months imprisoned in a room two paces wide. . . . They all want to make an end of me. We are dragged to inquiry after inquiry, the house is searched — basement, attic, trunks, your own icons and images. . . . And on the thirteenth of this month came the brigadier in uniform, the one who was guarding us, and told me to go to the Medresse jail, where they put the criminals."

This time he could not "come to an understanding" with God. Times had changed. He was taken to Medresse and was beaten and humiliated there. He was given a trial that was a parody of justice and was condemned to death. This sentence was changed to one of imprisonment, and finally he was set at liberty on September 2, 1854. There is nothing much left of Makryannis except his courage and his pride. He will speak to no one except God and his younger children. His house and his garden are now in ruins. The last sound of his voice — the last news we ever hear of him — seems to come from very far away. One could imagine that it is a whole race going to its own burial: "When they let me out of prison, I went to my ruined house and my wretched family. My wounds began to torment me. They did so last Easter and the Easter before. I went to the grotto in my garden to get a breath of air. I could hardly make my way there and had to lean heavily on my stick and on my will. And then they began to throw stones at me and human excrement. They said, 'Eat that, General Makryannis, and fill your belly with it, you who wanted to make a Constitution!' The blows they gave me opened up new wounds. My flesh is rotting; I have worms in me. I reported all this to the authorities and they would not listen to me. This lasted until the eve of the Day of our Savior. . . . And on the day itself they beat me up badly. I was left for dead and I could not feel whether I was dead or alive."

Not many years ago when I was searching in the

Ethnological Museum for any relics of Makryannis that I could find, I saw his death mask. The whole head was no bigger than a fist; it looked like a rotten apple or a sea pebble, deeply molded by the waves. This wretched object was all that had remained of the beautiful and noble figure of this magnanimous man.

3

Now, finally, I should like to express briefly my own opinion of the literary value of Makryannis's written work. You have heard some extracts. These are insufficient and inconclusive; but they will afford you some basis for judging the view that I hold. My view is this: Makryannis is the most important prose writer in modern Greek literature, if not the greatest — since we also have Papadiamantis.

Let us examine for a moment what we mean by "prose." Already for some decades poets have felt themselves free to dispense with the regular use of the outward and conventional marks of poetry — which are not in fact essential marks of poetry at all — such as rhyme and the old established meters. This does not mean that the distinction between prose and poetry has ceased to exist. On the contrary it has become more substantial. Poetry is a sort of dance; prose is, and ought to be, more like a marching step which is taking us somewhere. In the prose I am reading to you now I am trying to lead you somewhere. I am, as it were, walking at your side and trying to show you what Makryannis was like, just as if I were acting as your guide in some city which is unknown to you. But if I had to write a poem that would attempt to express Makryannis, it would not be at all the same thing. I might write three lines or three pages, and in what I wrote I should be concentrating upon my experience of the sufferings of my people; I should choose words which, according to my way of feeling, would arouse in you the same emotions that I felt when I first discovered Makryannis, and I might not even mention the name of Makryannis. In poetry the previous step is never lost in the subsequent one; on the contrary it remains fixed in the memory and stays intact in its place within the poem as a whole. But prose, as it moves forward, uses up the steps that it takes. In poetry the monad is the word; in prose it is the phrase, the paragraph, the page that we turn silently over. Its form and rhythm is the road we follow; its content is the falling into place of the things we see as we march forward. This is why the kind of prose which attempts to dance is bad prose — there is no worse prose than that which is called "poetic." The whole aim of a prose writer should be not beauty, but accuracy. And one cannot write accurately unless one has definite things to say which one believes to be worth saying. There must be, in short, a significant content.

The content of Makryannis's writing is the unending and tragic struggle of a man who, deeply rooted in the instincts of his race, is striving for freedom, justice and human dignity.

"Between Patras and Gastouni," he writes (the incident must have taken place in the 1830's), "there is a village, Mega Spileon. I stayed the night there. The villagers complained to me of the oppression they suffer from the monks. Whenever they get anything, the monks come and take it away from them. I said to them: 'If you are so oppressed here, why don't you leave this village and go to one of the many villages which are under government supervision?'

"The priest's wife then said: 'When the Turks came, we hid in the swamp water, so many souls, trying to save our lives. And the Turks came and took us. Our bodies were covered with leeches; they were eating us up. And the children were thrown in the water, floating like frogs, the water full of them. Some alive, some dying. And I was taken by the Turks and they slept with me, thirty-eight of them. And they finished me off, me and so many others. Why did we have to suffer all this? For this country of ours. And where is justice now? We cannot find it anywhere. Nothing but fraud and deception.'

"She was crying with bitter tears. I tried to comfort her. Misery overcame me and I too started to cry."

He fought, he struggled, he believed, he crippled himself, he became disillusioned and angry. But, as is shown by his rough writing, he remained upright to the end. He was a man of man's dimensions, neither a superman nor a worm. And really one of the graces of Makryannis which fills the heart with joy is this feeling that he never fails to give us — the feeling that we have at our side an experienced guide, and such a very human one, who is a measure for things and for people. This feeling has been deeply implanted in the Greek spirit ever since that faraway time when Oedipus made an end of the Sphinx and her world of nightmares by uttering the one word "Man."

The free man, the just man, the man who is the "measure" of life; if there is one basic idea in Hellenism, it is this one. It is born in the dawning of Greek thought; then it receives in the work of Aeschylus its full and firm extension. Whoever goes beyond the measure is guilty of "hubris," and "hubris" is the worst thing that can befall a man. To use Makryannis's expression, we Greeks have for a very long time been insisting on the "we" and not on the "I." Because whenever the "I" attempts to overcome the "we," then will fall the thunderbolt of "Ate," the stern fate that provides for the balance and equilibrium of the universe. All our ancient tragedy is full of images of this thought. And the image that I contemplate with the greatest emotion of all is to be found in *The Persians*. Xerxes, according to the old story, was defeated because he was guilty of "hubris," because he performed the outrageous act of flogging the sea. And so his ruin came to him from the sea, from this element that, although always tormented, never stops striving towards a balance, towards a "measure."

At the beginning of the Revolution, in Arta, Makryannis overhears one of the local beys speaking to his friends. He is careful to note the words:

"Pashas and beys, we shall be destroyed, destroyed! For this war is not with Moscow nor with the English nor the French. We have wronged the Greek infidel and taken away his wealth and his honor. And this darkened his eyes and he rose up in arms. And this Sultan, this beast of burden, does not know what is happening. He is deceived by those around him."

The cause of the Greek Revolution and of the ruin of the Turks is expressed by Makryannis in one sentence which he puts into the mouth of an enemy. It is just as when Aeschylus makes the enemy speak of their rout at Salamis. "We shall be destroyed, because we did wrong." If we want to understand the ancient Greeks, it is always into the soul of our own people that we should look. These words were spoken in 1821. Makryannis stores them up in his memory and sets them down years later, about 1829, after he has been through all the experiences of this bitter struggle. Behind his every act and behind his every statement, these words are lurking. They are present in his mind during the conversation he has with the French Admiral de Rigny when Makryannis is preparing to go into action at Myloi:

"As I was preparing our positions at Myloi, de Rigny came to see me. He says: 'What are you doing here? These positions are weak. What sort of war are you going to wage on Ibrahim from here?'

"I say to him: 'The positions are weak and we are weak. But the God who protects us is strong, and in these weak positions we shall show what our fortune is. And if we are few to be fighting against the masses of Ibrahim, we are somehow consoled by the thought that we Greeks have always happened to be few. That from the beginning to the end, in ancient times and today, all the wild beasts have been trying to eat us up and have failed. They eat up some of us, but the yeast remains. And the few decide to die. And once they make this decision, it often happens that they win, but a few times they lose. Such is the position in which we are here today. And we shall see what our fortune is, we few against the mighty.' " *'Très bien!'* says the Admiral and he goes off." Such is the faith and confidence which Makryannis affords.

The second reason which leads me to believe that Makryannis is the most important of our writers in prose is the fact that I regard him as a great teacher of our language. Except for the fragmentary "Woman of Zante" of Solomos, I know of no other text that teaches us so much as the writings of Makryannis.

Once I happened to write an introduction to the poetry of Calvos. It seemed to me that one of the problems he raised was the question of linguistic expression, and I was reproached by some critics for having given so much attention to a secondary aspect of his work instead of concerning myself with those things which the poet himself had proclaimed so loudly and clearly (and which had so little need of commentary from anyone else). I am indeed concerned with language; because it is the material of every writer, not because I want to revert to the old "language question," which now seems to be settled for Greece. No man of letters now writes in anything except the spoken language; and I expect that when we return to our country even the official documents of state will be written in the living tongue. Consider how today, in these black years of subjugation, the whole clandestine press that circulates in Greece in the teeth of oppressors and expresses the free thought of the nation is written in the spoken idiom. If, however, the language problem seems to have been liquidated, we should not forget that there can be no writer of stature who is not a "lord" of the language and that he will acquire this quality not through dictionaries and syntax but through that real living nature which comes to him every moment in the breathing of his race. And in order to assimilate this nature, we should first get to know and make part of our lives texts like this one of Makryannis, texts which, in my opinion, have the power to cleanse.

Meaning, language; the meaning that wants to be expressed and the language which must give a form, a positive existence to the meaning and so allow it to escape from obscurity. This force and this counterforce, unified in the end, create the style. These two conflicting forces are the difficulties of a writer. Out of these a style — a "voice," as the ancients called it — gives and takes on shape. The word is made articulate. This is why through language alone, however well we may know it, we can only create fine phrases, like "chaff on the threshing floor," as the song says, but without the resistance and the weight of the matter which we have to articulate, we shall never achieve style. Style is the difficulty encountered when a man tries to express himself; style is the human effort; "style is the very man," as the wise saying goes. That is why Makryannis's style is so real. And so unique, because its difficulties are also unique.

When I was speaking of the physical appearance of Makryannis's manuscript, I told you that it looked like a building in which one could spell out the steps of a human effort. His writing is just the same — a building done by hand. In its every detail — in its intensity, its ease, its falterings — is revealed the presence of a man's overflowing vitality. Someone said, "The best way to judge a piece of writing is to look for the words that do not function." In Makryannis the percentage of non-functioning words is fantastically small, smaller than in any Greek prose with which I am acquainted. And in conclusion let me recall a sentence of Pirandello's which always comes to my mind when I have to judge a piece of writing: "There is a style of things and a style of words; and this is why Dante died in exile while Petrarch was crowned on the Capitol." Poets are sometimes strange soothsayers. I think that if that oversized *pagliaccio* of fascism had had time to notice that small sentence of his compatriot, he might not have met his deplorable end. He was ruined by the pomp of words, that tragic illusion. But politicians seldom have time to notice such details.

Certainly in Makryannis we find this style of things, this style of necessity, this style of effectiveness. We have never heard in Greece so lapidary a voice. And there is no question here of folklore. The voice of Makryannis is a branch of that stalwart tree which gave us the *Erotocritos*, the *Sacrifice of Abraham*,* which gave us our popular songs and (I express my humble opinion for what it is worth) gave us also the greatest artist we have produced since the ancient Greeks, Domenicos Theotocopoulos — El Greco.

* Seventeenth-century drama of religious inspiration. Both poems are from the period of "The Cretan Renaissance," and in both are to be found splendid modern Greek lines.

MAKRYANNIS

This was what I had to tell you about Makryannis, the illiterate who traveled the road of a great life, who with such pains and effort set down on paper the things seen by his conscience. He is a surefooted messenger of the long and unbroken tradition of the people, which, because it is so deeply rooted in him, can teach us not just through one man's voice but in the voice of many, and can tell us what we are and how we are in our deepest selves. It tells us that his anger, his pain, his tragedy are not private affairs of his own, but concern all of us; they are affairs of yours, of mine, of all of us; they are affairs in which all of us together, the living and the dead, have our individual and our joint share and responsibility. He comes to whisper to us that our beauties and ornaments and riches, which we thought so valuable, are clean gone, worn out and turned to corruption; they can serve no purpose but to burden us and weigh us down, as in the case of the tragic Phaedra in her despair.

He comes to whisper this, at least to the intellectuals.

Ever since the eve of the First World War, the intellectual workers of Europe (and I mean those who have produced something significant) have been conscious that they live in a world that has been spoiled. This consciousness has led to violent intellectual revolutions, as appeared in the early postwar years. The whole period between the two wars can be characterized as a period of desperate research, internal excavation, a testing of the reality which surrounds us and which turns to dust under our fingers as we touch it. These efforts have led to a blank wall, to silence. There was in this situation the feeling of a deep sense of sin. And on this waste land — to use a characteristic title of those years — a new generation of the young attempted to build their world. The Spanish Civil War, which was the beginning of this present war, gave them the opportunity to leave behind their last messages.

Since the Spanish Civil War, we find nothing. It is no exaggeration to say that there is an intellectual blackout in Europe. This war, unlike the last one, is no time for artistic creativeness. All we can do is to assess our past and our present and wait for the dawn which will not fail to come. All we can do is to talk with friends and strangers, our comrades; to be on the lookout for the messages which they and our true intellectual ancestors can give us, to clear our conscience from temporary illusions; to believe that the great agony of the present moment must lead to a great day of resurrection, to see to it that we make ourselves worthy of that day; and to do our duty — "Poem of Duty" was the title of one of the great poems of Solomos. This resurrection cannot but be a resurrection of the life of man, in its most serious sense. As such it must put an end to the atrocities, the gagging, the prisons, the hypocrisies. It must be so; otherwise, alas, all that we live through today will have been lived through in vain. It must be so; otherwise the world will sink into a state of living death. And if what we believe in and what we are striving for does come to be, then it is very probable that in our country, where the values of man first saw the light, enlightened and educated people will understand (because they will be truly enlightened and truly educated) that the culture and discipline of their soul can be greatly aided by such works as this one of Makryannis, which is, I believe, the conscience of a whole nation — a testament of supreme value.

IV

Antoniou:
Our Seafaring Friend

Now that D. I. Antoniou has decided to publish some of his poems, I cannot help thinking back to that autumn evening, years ago, when he suddenly appeared before me in my office in London. He had unloaded his cargo, perhaps of grain, and was on his way to Cardiff for coal. After the long voyages to the River Plate he had a few quiet hours and they were filled with the uncertainty of the fog and the presence of a man who was not yet his friend. He was simple, with a look fixed on an imaginary margin to the left or to the right of us, circumspect and sure of himself when he wanted something. He carried with him that rather vague feeling which we love in those very few people who help us to live in our land, and which differentiates us, if difference there is, from other nations in the world. I should venture to call it the bitter cancer of Hellenism.

We went out into the empty streets of the becalmed city. On the wet pavement we could see, painted in multicolored crayons, the figure of Christ, with a discolored crimson forehead and heart, the portrait of Baldwin with a pipe in his mouth, and next to him a mermaid entangled in her

---

Written as a review in 1936.

own tail. We talked about the Black Sea, about that invincible force which drives people from the land to the sea, and from the sea to the land, and about the misfortunes of our race. . . . Now that I look again at these poems and see them in the impersonal face of typography, these poems that were originally written on the backs of innumerable packs of Greek cigarettes, I cannot help thinking back to these first conversations of ours, held as the lights of the advertisements embroidered the skin of the fog, like tattooing on a sailor's body. It is the same voice, the voice spoken from seaport after seaport and that has come back, all the way to our bucolic Athens. The same voice, which sometimes reaches the point of stammering, of one who balances the scales of sentiment, confronting his own fate with the fates of others which are far away and strange. Even though the factual element is sometimes nonexistent. For poetry facts are always a beginning, a starting point, submerged in some place which no one knows about, and the more deeply submerged, the better. Endless days, just as there is no end to the coal loaded under a leaden light, days spent on the bridge between sea and sky, as the ship rolls and struggles in the waves; seaports with all the bitterness of harbors, with the disenchantment of a desire finally accomplished after forty days of effort and hardship; smiles of exotic places, lighting up momentarily, like the dawn of our native island — all these shades and colors, which we either see instantly or may never see at all, are to be found in the poetry of our seafaring friend. They are to be found just as we might find them if we were reading them in the pages of a logbook, or if we were suddenly to see under the light, looking through a door that had been left open, the face of a sailor, solemn and submissive, as the ship carries us away from the things we love.

Since then Antoniou has left the oceans and left the ship "with the name of the blond hero." His later voyages were in the White Sea of the Aegean. But there was no alteration in his habit of filling up his cabin with empty cigarette boxes covered with verses on every available surface. "My bottles in the sea," he used to call them. One day I remember his whispering to me, between orders to the steersman, his verses. We had our course fixed towards the moon. The sea was calm and Greece was sleeping. Nothing disturbed this rhythmical abolition of time. After a long silence I heard him whisper again, a line from Mallarmé: *Fuir! là-bas fuir! Je sens que les oiseaux sont ivres* . . .

And we thought of that distant night in the fog when, speaking of the coal that had to be loaded next morning, we agreed that, after all, at the bottom of every coal pit there is always a white horse, and that the duty of every one of us is to find his white horse, at any cost.

These poems are the white horse of our seafaring friend.

V

Dialogue on Poetry: What
Is Meant by Hellenism?

I STILL feel an affection for teaching. This, I think, is due largely to the fact that in the days of my youth, I was aware of a sense of deprivation, when, like others I imagine, I was trying to find my way by myself and experienced that condition of alienation and bereavement known to the self-taught. But apart from this personal reason, I find that this particular style, this method of communication, which presupposes a circle of devoted disciples following the thought of a master both older and more experienced than they, has in itself a peculiar and enviable grace. And I am sorry that teaching in our country has distorted and disfigured so many values, thus preventing the formation of a steady, robust and free didactic style which could well be one of the foundation stones for an enduring modern Greek tradition.

This affection (which would lead me to say, for instance, that I am not at all averse to didactic poetry) caused me to read with the greatest interest

---

This *Dialogue* is a short part of a long discussion which took place in 1938 and 1939 between the author and Mr. Constantinos Tsatsos, then professor of philosophy at Athens University. In its present form it cannot, obviously, give a clear and fair image of the whole discussion from both sides. The argument started from an article of Mr. Tsatsos which appeared in the periodical *Propylaea* in 1938. Seferis replied in the literary review *New Letters*.

the essay by Constantine Tsatsos entitled "Before the Beginning." In this essay the writer, with the help of sublime philosophy, tries to show young people how to find that imaginary and ideal point of view from which they will be able to gain the full conception of a worthy intellectual personality; a point like that sought by Archimedes to provide him with the basis from which he would be able to move the earth. Indeed Archimedes' "Give me a place to stand" is the motto of this study in the organization of the personality of intellectual man. And since the intellectual at all times has also to deal with the vital problem of poetry, the writer devotes part of his essay to this subject. I feel quite incompetent to deal with the other questions which he raises, but on this question of poetry I shall have a few things to say.

Mr. Tsatsos starts his reflections with a comment on the "avant-garde movement in our very recent literature," as he calls it. His criticisms of this movement come under a variety of heads. In examining them, I am not taking on the role of a champion; I am not much interested in "schools." However since I happen to be a "minor" poet myself, who has been, on various occasions, credited with quite a lot of contradictory experimentation outside his main field, I am all the more interested in the way in which the public reacts to the works of poetry that are set before it and how it is taught to understand them.

DIALOGUE ON POETRY: WHAT IS MEANT BY HELLENISM?

I hold the view that the best way in which theoreticians can help to advance the understanding of art is in trying to form a public that can sometimes show a spark of emotional perception that is without prejudice and without those purely intellectual reactions that can be observed so often, not so much in the people as among the overargumentative and formalistically educated members of our upper classes. What I have in mind is a public capable of approaching a work of art in that state of "good faith" which we may be in when saying our prayers or (if this example is too obscure) in the state of mind of simple people listening to an old legend or of children listening to a fairy tale. And by this I do not mean that I am demanding a state of primitive simplicity. The critic has an important task to perform in building up, organizing and making people familiar with intellectual values that are still vague and scattered; and the more acumen he shows, the better the result. But what most of our critics do is simply to create a state of personal litigation between the public and the work of art which it comes to see or hear. And no one, certainly, enters the kingdom of heaven in this way. One may engage in interminable discussions and still not have any aesthetic feeling at all. So when I am told that the "avant-gardists" consider praiseworthy everybody who has found a new form of expression, without bothering to inquire into the more fundamental problems of poetry, even the most unimportant of poets may be tempted to exclaim: "How nice life would be if the critics had not taken such care to cultivate what is probably an innate tendency in the public to feel that one's aesthetic task is over, once one has managed to paste a label on the work that is put in front of one! How nice life would be if all these gentlemen devoted their attention simply and solely to finding out the poetic essence of my poem! As it is, they are looking for such a lot of other things which have never concerned me at all."

And my critical friend is teaching them all the time to look for more and more things. Let us discuss them — if discuss we must.

2

THE young man who is studying this teaching will be asked first of all to consider whether "the opposition of logical and illogical elements within the poetic work" is legitimate or illegitimate. What I ask myself is — is there any real point in this opposition between the logical and illogical elements in poetry? Do we not detect it only when we are annoyed by something or when we fail to understand it — which is often the same thing?

Somewhere in his essay Mr. Tsatsos writes: "Real love is the love of the concrete." I agree. He adds: "The other form of inquisitiveness, which is still searching for its first foothold and which in our times is often and admiringly described as 'restlessness,' indicates only the awakening of the indolence of matter." This I can follow. He goes on: "True intellectuality consists of more than question marks, doubts, negations and inquiries which are in fact merely sophistical affectations." I still follow him, imagining that he is making a distinction and giving his preference to a given and a steady position, a hierarchical faith, as against a kind of confused restlessness. But I am startled and am quite at a loss to understand him when he ends up by saying that he accepts both the way of Dante treading within his circles, the *Gypsy* of Palamas,* and Marcel Proust, together with "every pathfinder of the absolute, provided that his wanderings are not dictated by the prevailing winds" in the various European capitals or by "the caprices of his individual psychosynthesis."

I try to understand. Dante may be accepted without question; he was a man totally disciplined in his faith and his love. But what, as something precise and steady, was the object of love in the *Gypsy* except Palamas's own spirit of restlessness? And what did Proust love other than the failures of his own memory and heart, that is to say the caprices of his psychosynthesis? And if we accept the position that in our investigation of the absolute there can also be a pure restlessness, then what happens to the concrete? I do not say that my learned friend is wrong; only that I am unable to follow him. He

* *The Dodecalogue of the Gypsy* (1907), a long poem by Kostes Palamas.

cannot even reply to me, like Julien Benda, "Monsieur, I am a metaphysician, not a littérateur." Benda I should understand. Not that it would ever cross my mind to assert that in the philosophy of Mr. Tsatsos and his friends the logical element is in the least undernourished. All that I can say is that they are formulating ideas which are difficult to grasp and are doing this with a technique which is to me forbidding.

Let us leave metaphysics alone. So far as poetry is concerned, there is an example which comes to mind. How much of the logical element is there in our folk songs? Some time ago I had occasion to comment on the following six lines:

> I kissed red lips and my own lips were dyed red.
> I wiped them with my handkerchief and it was dyed red.
> I washed it in the river and the river was dyed red.
> The shores were dyed red and the great sea.
> An eagle flew down to drink the water and his feathers were dyed red;
> Dyed red was half the sun and the full moon.

Let us suppose that we are not used to folk song and let us say that some unknown poet shows us for the first time a poem made of associated expressions of this sort. Would he not appear to us to be out of his mind? Because here the images follow a construction that is purely poetic, that is illogical, and this construction, in my view, is very far from being opposed to "the deeper principle of the Greek intellect" or to "Hellenic beauty." My opinion, of course, is not infallible and may be discussed further. . . .*

3

ON the other hand, how is it possible to lay down in advance what the frontiers of art are to be and to say that beyond a certain line art cannot exist, as seems to be the belief of those with whom I am conducting this discussion? I readily agree that art is a kind of pattern, a kind of rule, and an inexorable rule at that. But this rule has not been laid down by any abstract theory. It has been laid down by the whole series of great works of art which, with the passing of time, light our way with a light which is ever newer and ever steadier. For every work of art that comes to be added to the series affirms and at the same time modifies the meaning of the older masterpieces. Dante, for example, does not have the same meaning before and after Baudelaire, nor Racine before and after Valéry, nor the Elizabethans before and after T. S. Eliot. Thus we may establish a kind of correspondence between Homer and Vergil, Homer and Aeschylus, Aeschylus and Euripides, or, in our modern poetry, between Calvos and Cavafy. This is a living tradition and it is in this way — not solidified and unchangeable — that works of art live.

Mr. Tsatsos writes: "I once asked a theoretical

* Two pages are here omitted from the Greek edition. — R.W.

defender of this new movement, perhaps the most conscious of all of them, how the masterpieces of the past could be kept alive if every era has its own new aesthetic principles and forms which alone are fit to express it. Either, it would seem, the work of the past remains alive and equal to the newest works, and then the attempt to find new modes of form and new 'schools' becomes pointless; or else we are aesthetically more profoundly and more genuinely moved by the new works of art, in which case the old masterpieces, seen as an aesthetic 'good,' are losing their value."

It seems that the "theoretical defender" replied that the masterpieces of the past only moved him in a historical sense. What a singularly bad "defense"!

For there is no discrepancy between old and new works of art, none whatsoever. The great works of the past remain "aesthetically" distinct and emotionally near to us, and all the more so if there are new works constantly arriving to fortify their position. Perhaps we might be able to look at them "in a historical sense" if this constant renovation of art forms could be stopped, because in that case our aesthetic perception would have come to an end also. It is well known how our understanding of Villon or Shakespeare has been enlarged by the romantic movement, which was itself a "new school" attempting "new forms in art." Art is an endless continuity and solidarity, and no one who fails to recognize this can possibly claim to have an understanding of it.

This is why I am just as deeply grieved as are the critics with whom I am dealing by the ignorance which is prevalent among us; and I am in complete agreement when they say, "Gentlemen, read your classics; you can never read enough of them." But I am disturbed when I find them endlessly insisting on the existence of a chasm — which to me does not exist — separating and isolating the classics from the nonclassics, which in the final analysis means simply a division between good artists and bad artists or, in fact, between artists and those who are not artists at all. The little men, the ignorant, those who cannot stand on their own feet are all birds of a feather, whether they are imitating Pindar or Goethe or Baudelaire or Kostes Palamas or the surrealists. And if we consider how much bad art — I mean to say how much academic art — has been produced in the name of the classics, we should be all the more severe in our judgment on those very mediocre people who try to cling tight to the "eternal values" and who deform them like parasites that settle like a blight on perennial trees. And I am surprised when in this dispute between the ancients and the moderns — which is far from being a new thing — I find my friend Mr. Tsatsos putting all his weight onto the side of the ancients and having nothing but scorn for the moderns.

He writes: "There is a much greater difference

between Titian and Veronese, between da Vinci and Luini, between Corneille and Racine, between Hugo and Vigny, a much greater difference between true creators belonging to the same school and working with the same ideas and the same means than is to be found between two followers of two avant-garde schools which are in total opposition to each other."

Of course this is true if these two followers are both mediocre, since there is no greater leveler than mediocrity. However, if they are in fact mediocre, I wonder why we should give them such importance and compare them with Racine and Hugo, as if the innumerable mediocre imitators of Racine and Hugo were not in their case too all leveled down, as is shown by the oblivion into which they have sunk and which awaits, alas, our own mediocre writers. But Mr. Tsatsos does not mention this fact. Nor have I observed that he has even said that the same differentiation may be noticed among those who have been accused of being insane, sophisticated or affected. Mallarmé and Valéry worked with the same aesthetic data and very similar technique; yet the differences between their respective works are so great and obvious that it would be merely tiresome to enumerate them. In English literature the two major contemporary poets, T. S. Eliot and Ezra Pound, two close friends with the same aesthetic tendencies, made the same experiments, undertook the same discipline and were inspired by the same prototypes, yet they are totally different personalities. And since things are so, why should we not say to our imaginary young man: "My dear fellow, if you want to be somebody in this kingdom of the intellect, try to avoid mediocrity at every moment of your life, try to live in as close contact as you can with the higher spirits whom you will be fortunate enough to encounter. Work, dig down inside yourself, purify your spirit and go free."

But the friend with whom I am carrying on this discussion comes to the following conclusion: "The addition of one shadow, of one line to the continuity of an integrated and established tradition will show more originality than is to be found in all these fundamental upheavals. Because this additional shadow or line reveals a new intellectual personality, raises the work to a different initial point of departure and gives a basic support to its originality."

I do not agree. This shadow or this line may certainly show great originality, but may also show — as is the case with nearly all the French poetry of the eighteenth century — a quite insufferable mediocrity. And this is why I protest. But "ignorant awareness" as he calls it can be a nuisance and can play a great part in inducing us to put the unjust and the just into the same bag and to write that "Plato would have called these followers of the avant-garde movement 'affected' (*kompsoi*) as he called the sophists."

I do not know what Plato would have called them. Possibly, looking more closely at what they were trying to do, he might have used a more complimentary adjective, perhaps one of those which he uses in the *Phaedrus*. I should like, however, to insist that it is not fair to create confusion in the minds of the young by advising them to beware of new devils when all the time there are so many old devils living and thriving unopposed. Nor is it right to judge ideas we do not accept by the products of their least distinguished exponents, while we throw a veil of silence over the defects of enthusiasts supporting views which we happen to like.

4

My friend has another type of exhortation. This concerns the "hellenicity" of a work of art — a theme which has never ceased to attract attention and inquiry, and one which is still very much alive, since it involves two or three basic problems in our Greek intellectual life. But before I set down a few observations on this subject I should like to look rather more closely at a preliminary matter — our heritage from the older writers. "Among the writers of the past," writes Mr. Tsatsos, "the effort to express the Greek soul, the Greek soil and its history, is extremely intense and sometimes exaggeratedly exclusive. At the same time the organ of expression, the language, is tended by them, enriched and polished with care and with affection. Their rhythms, their moods of expression were formed by an intensive exploitation of the possibilities of the treasures to be found in our folklore. On the contrary the works of our avant-garde . . ." and so forth.

Now let us see. I think that we should all agree if we said, broadly speaking, that before the "avant-garde" which he presumably has in mind came the generation that reached maturity long before the 1914 war; there followed the generation which might have been described, though not very accurately, as the generation of Karyotakis.* It was against this generation that the Thirties in general reacted.

The first generation could show an impressive array of important writers, both in prose and poetry. Many of these played an important part in the struggle for the use of the demotic language. I say many, not all, because one of the most important among them, Cavafy, stayed outside this movement, as did some of his immediate disciples. But, again speaking generally, I think that with the passage of years the time has now come for us, when we estimate the writers of this generation, to make a distinction between their own personal aims — their aesthetic aims — and the general movement towards the use of the demotic language. Otherwise we shall be in danger of failing to judge them with a proper impartiality. The movement in favor of demotic was in the first place a group movement

* Kostas Karyotakis, born Tripoli (Peloponnese) in 1896, died Preveza 1928. An influential poet. He committed suicide.

for the use of our national means of expression; then, more subtly, for the realization of the true and genuine outlook and idiosyncrasy of the Greek race. The movement must be described as a complex system of ideas which has sometimes had a radical and profound influence on our writers, but often its influence is merely superficial; certainly it was a complex of ideas quite independent of the aesthetic aims of the generation which we are discussing. Between 1897 and 1914 we have a great number of works which under a façade of folklore are clearly foreign in inspiration, just as we have a great number of literary books which, though they may be called very good studies of folklore, have no aesthetic value at all. This movement has exerted a deep influence not only on our literature but on every aspect of our national life. We cannot adequately honor it, nor can we adequately honor literature, unless we make the distinction which I have noted. There is nothing to be gained by a confusion of ideas. If we make this distinction we shall see that a great many of the qualities which Mr. Tsatsos finds in the writings of the older generation — expression of the Hellenic spirit (I should prefer "the spirit of the people"), enrichment of the language, exploitation of our folklore — are certainly attributable to this movement when they are concerned with the surface of these writings. But if we look deeper, we shall find that the best writers of that generation never hesitated for a moment

DIALOGUE ON POETRY: WHAT IS MEANT BY HELLENISM?

about accepting lavishly influences that came from abroad. "Imitation," wrote Kostes Palamas in 1898, "is the great rule of societies and of literature." And again, "Every day our younger poets appear to grasp more clearly the fact that the only patriotism compatible with a poetic dignity is the conscientious and disinterested application to the love of art . . . that the Greek poet, who has before him the example of his immortal ancestors, must be first of all a human being and that true national poetry is poetry without a country and poetry in its highest intensity."

I do not think that I am exaggerating in the least when I say that this was the aesthetic credo of the best poets in the generation of Palamas on the subject which we are now discussing. And it was along these lines that they tried to "discover new facets of Greek life." And if Palamas absorbed and used everything that he possibly could from our own intellectual treasures, he remained also wide open to the intellectual "developments" that were going on abroad. In the same way Gryparis* made use both of Parnassianism and of Symbolism in order to express himself, and we know how much Black Forest there is to be found in the works of Hadjipoulos.†

Even the "mixed language" (and here I am

---

* John Gryparis (1872–1942), a poet and a scholar who is widely known for his translations of ancient Greek tragedies.
† Kostas Hadjipoulos (1869–1920). Poet and novelist.

thinking of Cavafy) is a legacy from that generation. This reached its zenith (and in a much less carefully polished way) during the time of the first postwar generation, when the struggle for the demotic language had degenerated and Karyotakis had come on the scene. Probably Mr. Tsatsos has these people in mind when he writes, "Young people seem to have dulled their love and knowledge of the language and there is no protest when demotic and 'purist' Greek are juxtaposed." At that time this mixture or juxtaposition was not the real trouble. What was much more terrible was the fact that nobody seemed to care about the style of expression at all. It was a period when all in chorus, critics and poets alike, were demanding spontaneity and disregarding anything else. It was against this dissolution of principles that the poets who appeared after 1930 reacted, sometimes, perhaps, too self-consciously.

5

THIS question, however, is much more interesting if considered under its general aspects. When Mr. Tsatsos writes of the Hellenic character of literary works; when he declares that genuine poetic works "should be the discovery of new aspects of Greek life and should not be a retreat from this life"; when he says that these works "should be entirely free of foreign 'movements' " and that "they should spring from the selfsame source of Hellenic life,

DIALOGUE ON POETRY: WHAT IS MEANT BY HELLENISM?

determined always by the original disposition of a consciousness that lives the only possible genuine life, a life with it roots in this earth and this soil of ours"; when I read passages such as these I assume that we are to regard the "Hellenism" of a work of art as a special aesthetic criterion by which it may be condemned or approved, quite irrespectively of its other qualities or defects.

I cannot accept such a rule and prefer rather those views of Palamas which I have already noted.

"Hellenism" as applied to a work of art is a big word to use. A big word and a fine word. But if we want to pin down exactly what is meant by it, we shall find it a difficult and dangerous word to use in this context. Those who agitated for the artificially "purist" language aimed just at this; they sought for just this kind of "Hellenism." With touching obstinacy, with sweat and toil they tried to purify the national language from the stains of "barbarism" and hoped that slowly but surely we should attain once more the language and the art of Sophocles and Plato. And ,their reward was what might have been expected — a destruction and a drying up of Hellenism's fairest and truest streams. I shall confine myself to this example and pass over the many others that might be given, the innumerable and very harmful incongruities that were put forward in defense of "Hellenism." This is why I used the word "dangerous," because we run the risk, as was the case of the purists, of destroying in the name of "Hellenism" those values which are most purely Hellenic. But the opposite may happen too; and this is why I used the adjective "difficult." We may also, in the confidence that we are "hellenizing," come under the sway of values which are not Hellenic at all or only remotely so.

Since the time of Alexander the Great we have scattered our Hellenism far and wide. We have sown it throughout the world: "As far as Bactria we took it, as far as the Indians," as Cavafy says. And this vast diaspora was to have a significant result. Hellenism was worked upon, reformed and revivified, right down to the time of the Renaissance, by personalities who were sometimes Greek and sometimes not. And after that time, which marks the enslavement of the Greek race, it was shaped by personalities who were not Greek at all and who worked outside the Greek area. And we should remember that it was in this period that were created those great works which crystalized the form of the civilization which we know today as European.

This civilization, which is basically an offspring of the values of Hellenism, was created neither by us nor by our immediate ancestors. Our immediate ancestors preserved the treasures of the past and, at the fall of Byzantium, left, as Palamas says, holding

>   heavy jars full
>   of the ashes of their ancestors

and so brought the seed of Hellenism to the West, where it prospered, finding a free and suitable soil. But as for a Renaissance made by us, however much certain indications may lead us to suppose that it would have been something different from one made by the Europeans, it is nevertheless true that a Renaissance made by Greeks, whether we like it or not, simply did not occur. No Greek had any decisive or immediate influence at that time on the trends which were taking shape in the West as a result of the contact with Greek values. There was no one — with the exception of Domenicos Theotocopoulos (El Greco), himself long underrated, who was not only a vehicle but a creator as well. This was how things stood until the time of the awakening of the race. Then, just as is done today, the best among us studied in or went to the West and tried to bring back to liberated Greece the heritage that had left our country in order to be preserved. But this heritage was not a matter of lifeless gold; it was a living thing that had fertilized its surroundings and taken root and borne fruit. And through these functions it gradually came to be a general and abstract framework inside which many powerful intelligences came to find their places, each completely different from the others and more consonant with their own selves than with anything else. Dante's Ulysses, Shakespeare's Venus and Adonis, Racine's Phèdre and Hölderlin's Hyperion, apart from their worldwide significance and value,

ON THE GREEK STYLE

belong basically to the times and the races of their creators; their Hellenic subject matter is, as motivation, something external and superficial. We, however, with most legitimate and commendable motives, burning, as we were, with the desire to bring back to Greece everything that was Hellenic and seeing signs of Hellenism everywhere, brought back, without looking more deeply into the matter, countless foreign values which in fact had nothing to do with our own land at all.

We all know the buildings of the modern Academy in Athens, an example of pseudoclassical architecture. But we do not realize that very often when we are speaking of the "Hellenism" of some work of art, we are really speaking about the buildings of the Academy. "And what should be done?" I shall be asked. I said that Hellenism is something difficult. And this comes about because if, in the realm of the intellect, European Hellenism was created (and, who knows, perhaps in our days is dying), our own "Greek Hellenism," if I may be permitted so to call it, has not yet been created and has not yet recovered its tradition. Sometimes, in the mature works of our writers we begin to feel it, when studying, for example, the deepest features of Calvos, the verses of Solomos, the agony of Palamas, the nostalgia of Cavafy. In the London National Gallery there is a small canvas of Theotocopoulos — El Greco — the portrait of a saint, a painting not more than fifteen inches high. More than ten years have passed since I saw this picture for the first time. I cannot forget the overwhelming impression of "Hellenism" that was conveyed to me by this minor example of the great master's work. I still remember two brush strokes on the shoulders; "like Cretan fifteen-syllable lines," said the friend who was with me. We were young then. Sometimes there is a foreknowledge of this "Greek Hellenism" among some of the best of us, "for wise men perceive what is approaching." But before we can say that we can see its face clearly, many great works will have to be created and many men, great and small alike, will have to work and to struggle. For this particular Hellenism will only show its face when the Greece of today has acquired its own real intellectual character and features. And its characteristics will be precisely the synthesis of all the characteristics of all true works of art which have ever been produced by Greeks. Meanwhile, let us remind the younger generation that if the movement towards the use of the demotic language is for us one of the major events in our national history, this is because, above all, it symbolizes the first step and turning point towards the truth. And let us advise them to seek truth, just as the first advocates of demotic did, not asking how they can be Greeks, but confident in the fact that, since they are Greeks, the works created out of their souls cannot be anything else but Hellenic.

If I am right, the whole question is this: how profoundly and how truly can a Greek confront his own self and that nature of his which must inevitably be part of the greater nature which is Hellenic? And here, of course, the ways become darker and exact prescriptions are of no help. I should like, however, before I end to be allowed to quote a passage of Alain which seems to me singularly illuminating. "The union of the poet with nature," he writes, "is elsewhere, in a direction that is not the one immediately expected. It is in the submission to the laws of his own voice, of his own breathing, of his own way of walking — which are our own too. . . . On the other hand a mere versifier tries to describe and he achieves nothing. In vain he copies objects, in vain he copies his own thoughts and feelings. Because by this procedure form derives from thinking; it is not poetry, it is industry. . . . The sincerity that belongs to a poet does not lie in his intellect, but rather in the confidence which he puts entirely in his own blind nature which joins in harmony with the greater Nature in a form of walking or of dancing."

It is in this same spirit of confidence that one will be Hellenic.

I feel that perhaps people may interpret what I have been saying as implying that the only viewpoint which I accept is that of agnosticism. This is not so. What I am saying is that contemporary Greece, attempting, as she is, to find the right attitude towards her ancient tradition, which is known to her exclusively through foreign sources; beginning only now to become conscious even of her recent history, and forced to import the greater part of her intellectual requirements, presents a kind of intellectual landscape in which there are scarcely any discernible landmarks and all around lie tracts of barren and largely unknown country. As for the artist who wishes to live in this land, he is sometimes, if I may say so, very cruelly isolated among these barren tracts, parched up, and withered away. And this is why we see so many at the starting point and so few reaching the end of the course. And since his position is so difficult, let us not make his task more complicated still by burdening him with theories that lead nowhere.

But I am forgetting the "avant-garde." It is not my intention to defend them. Some of them are young poets who have done a good job that is not in the least contrary to "the deeper principle of the Hellenic spirit." All they want is to be left alone to work as well as they can.

As for my friend Mr. Tsatsos, I know that fundamentally it would not be difficult for him and me to come to an agreement. But I doubt whether I should be able to agree with the young students who will listen to his teachings. It is for both these reasons that I have been so loquacious, and "I'm not usually like this," as Makryannis would say.

VI
Letter on "The *Thrush*"

At the end of 1949 my friend George Katsimbalis asked me to write him a letter that might help the well-intentioned reader to read my poem "The Thrush" more easily.* The fact was that at that time this poem appeared to be utterly incomprehensible. I sat down, and in the lighthearted way which one has when writing to a friend, I wrote out for him a kind of scenario. "So," I wrote, "it may well be that some day 'The Thrush' will be shown as a film." A few people understood what I was driving at; others turned my words against me or hastened to ascribe to me inconceivable intentions; they thought I was trying to give a definitive interpretation of a poem or, more precisely, to complete a poem of mine with a piece of prose. I have now reread this letter and I think that both the first and the second class of readers have already derived whatever good or bad they could from it. Here I am reprinting only the concluding passages, since they contain a few of those more general thoughts that, I think, have their place in this book.

My dear George . . .

Any explanation of a poem is, I think absurd. Everyone who has the slightest idea of how an artist

---
* "The Thrush" is given in its entirety beginning on page 109.

works knows this. He may have lived long, he may have acquired much learning, he may have been trained as an acrobat. When, however, the time comes for him to create, the mariner's compass that directs him is the sure instinct that knows, above all, how to bring to light or to sink in the twilight of his consciousness the things (or, as I should prefer to say, the tones) that are necessary, that are unnecessary or that are just sufficient for the creation of this something: the poem. He does not think of these materials; he fingers them, he weighs them, he feels their pulse. When this instinct is not mature enough to show the way, the most fiery sentiment may become disastrous and useless, like frozen ratiocination; it will be able to do nothing but stammer. Poetry, from a technical point of view, may be defined as "the harmonic word" — with the greatest possible emphasis on the term "harmonic," in the sense of a conjunction, cohesion, correlation, opposition of one idea to another, of one emotion to another. Once I spoke of a "poetic ear"; I meant the ear that can discern such things as these.

I think that this kind of hearing, as I define it, is less common in Greece now than it was among the Ionians* in the time of Solomos; less common also than is usual in present-day Europe. Perhaps this is due to lack of care, perhaps to our linguistic

---

* The inhabitants of the Ionian Islands, which had never been subjected to the Turks, had a higher cultural level than the liberated Greeks of the mainland.

anarchy, perhaps to the fact that here the evolution of our poetry has been too rapid and nobody has really been able to keep up with it. Generally speaking, in Greece there is less response than one might expect from the trained listeners to poetry. To this, I think, must be attributed the fact that we observe so many and such gross mistakes in our poetical judgments. However it may be, one needs an ear to hear poetry; the rest is just chatting round the fire at Christmas, as I am doing now.

I think of this as I try to understand how it came about that in "The Thrush" I had to substitute Socrates for Tiresias. My first answer is that I saw elsewhere the tones that were necessary for the ensemble that I was attempting to complete; the idea of the Theban never even occurred to me. Then — autobiographically — because the *Apology* is one of the books that has most influenced me in my life; perhaps because my generation has grown up and lived in this age of injustice. Thirdly, because I have a very organic feeling that identifies humaneness with the Greek landscape.

I must say that this feeling of mine, which is shared, I think, by many others, is often rather painful. It is the opposite of that state of ceasing to exist, of the abolition of the ego, which one feels in face of the grandeur of certain foreign landscapes. I should never use such adjectives as "grand" or "stately" for any of the Greek landscapes I have in mind. It is a whole world: lines that come and go; bodies and features, the tragic silence of a "face." Such things are difficult to express, and I can see the boys getting ready to take up the mocking chorus: "the graverobber of Yannopoulos." However it may be, it is my belief that in the Greek light there is a kind of process of humanization; I think of Aeschylus not as the Titan or the Cyclops that people sometimes want us to see him as, but as a man feeling and expressing himself close beside us, accepting or reacting to the natural elements just as we all do. I think of the mechanism of justice which he sets before us, this alternation of Hubris and Ate, which one will not find to be simply a moral law unless it is also a law of nature. A hundred years before him Anaximander of Miletus believed that "things" pay by deterioration for the "injustice" they have committed by going beyond the order of time. And later Heraclitus will declare: "The sun will not overstep his measures; if he does, the Erinyes, the handmaids of Justice, will find him out."

The Erinyes will hunt down the sun, just as they hunted down Orestes; just think of these cords which unite man with the elements of nature, this tragedy that is in nature and in man at the same time, this intimacy. Suppose the light were suddenly to become Orestes? It is so easy, just think: if the light of the day and the blood of man were one and the same thing? How far can one stretch this feeling? "Just anthropomorphism," people say, and they pass

LETTER ON "THE THRUSH"

on. I do not think it is as simple as that. If anthropomorphism created the *Odyssey,* how far can one look into the *Odyssey?*

We could go very far; but I shall stop here. We arrived at the light. And the light cannot be explained; it can only be seen. The rest of this scenario may be filled in by the reader — after all, he has to do something too; but let me first recall the last words of Anticleia to her son:

> The soul, like a dream, flutters away and is gone.
> But quickly turn your desire to the light
> And keep all this in your mind.
> [*Odyssey* XI, 222–224]

Something like this was told to me by that small ship, sunk in the harbor at Poros, that in the happy days used to sail on errands to supply the naval establishment.

I hope that all this has shown you that I am a monotonous and obstinate sort of man who, for the last twenty years, has gone on saying the same things over and over again — things that are not even his own. . . .

And now, since we have forgotten about it entirely, do me the favor to read, as though it were a Christmas carol, the poem called "The Thrush."

Happy New Year,
G.S.

Ankara
27 December 1949

VII

The *Thrush*

"Shortlived offspring of a cruel daemon and a hard fate, why do you force me to speak of things which it would be better for you not to know."
—Silenus to Midas

1
The House Near the Sea

The houses that I had they took from me. It happened
The times were out of joint. Wars, waste and exiles.
Sometimes the hunter gets the birds of passage,
Sometimes he does not get them. There was in my time
Good hunting. Burst of fire took a heavy toll.
The others turn round and round or go mad in the
    shelters.

Do not speak to me of the nightingale, do not speak of
    the lark,
Do not speak of the little wagtail
Who with his tail writes figures on the light.
I do not know a great deal about houses:
They have their own temper; that is all I know.
New at first, like babies
Who play in gardens with the tassels of the sun,
They do their embroideries with colored shutters
And doors brilliantly shining on the screen of the day.
When the architect has finished, then they change,
They wrinkle up, they smile, or again grow obstinate
With those who stayed behind and with those who
    left,

ON THE GREEK STYLE

With others who would return there if they could,
Or who have become lost now that this had
    happened —
The world become a limitless inn for strangers.

I do not know a great deal about houses;
I remember their joy and their sorrow
Sometimes, when I stand still;
                              and also
At times, near the sea, in rooms stripped naked
With a single iron bedstead and nothing that is mine,
Looking at the evening spider I call to mind
That such a one is getting ready to come, that they
    adorn him
In clothes of white and black with colored jewels,
And around him is the slow speech of respected ladies,
With their gray hair and their dark lace; —
That he gets ready to come to say goodbye to me.
Or a woman deep-girdled, with glancing eyes,
Returning home from harbors of the south,
Smyrna, Rhodes, Syracuse, Alexandria,
From cities closed like shutters closed in the heat,
With perfume of golden fruit, and aromatic herbs,
That she is climbing the stairs without paying attention
To those who have gone to sleep underneath the stairs.

You find houses get obstinate easily, when you strip
    them naked.

II

The Lustful Elpenor

I saw him yesterday stop by the door,
Down from my window. It was round about

THE THRUSH

Seven o'clock and there was a woman with him.
He had the look of Elpenor just before
He fell and broke; and yet he was not drunk.
He was speaking very quickly, and the woman
Looked in an absent way towards the gramophones;
She stopped him occasionally to say a word or two
And then she would look away impatiently
To where they were frying fish. Like a cat looks.
He whispered with a fag-end in his lips:
"Listen again to this. I have seen by moonlight
Sometimes the statues leaning over like reeds
In the middle of living fruit — the statues,
And the flame becomes a dewy oleander,
The flame that burns the man, I mean to say."

"A trick of the light . . . the effect of the night shadows."

"The night perhaps: which opened, a blue pomegranate,
Dark breasts, filling you full of stars,
Cutting down time.
     But all the same the statues
Sometimes do bend, and they deal out desire
Into two parts, like a peach shared, and the flame
Becomes a kiss on the limbs, a sobbing of breath
And then a cool leaf the wind carries away.
They bend, they become light with a human weight.
You cannot forget it."

    "The statues are in the museum."

"No, it is you they hunt. Why can't you see?
I mean the statues with their broken limbs
And faces from another time you have never

ON THE GREEK STYLE

    Seen and yet you know them.
                                It is like
At the end of your youth you happen to be in love
With a woman who has kept her beauty. Holding
Her naked body in the noon, always
You fear the memory that surges up
To your embrace, you fear the kiss betraying you
To other beds which now are in time past,
And yet, for all that, there are ghosts might stalk there
Easily, so easily, and bring to life
Images to the mirror, bodies that were once,
And all the lust they had then.
                              It is like
Coming back from a foreign land you chance to open
An old chest that for long has been locked up;
And there you find bits and pieces of the dresses
You wore in lovely times, in lighted revels
Of many colors, mirrored, which all fade,
And remains only the perfume of the absence
Of a young face.
                     Oh it is true; the fragments
Are not the statues. You are yourself the remains.
They haunt you with their strange virginity
At home or office, at the big receptions
For honored people, in your unconfessed
Terror of sleep. They speak of what you wish
Had never happened, or could happen years
After your death. Difficult, because — "

                        "The statues are in the museum.
Good night."

    "Because the statues are no more fragments.
We are. The statues lightly bend. . . . Good night."

THE THRUSH

At this they separated and he took
The upper road that leads towards the Bear.
And she went forward to the lighted beach
Where the wave is drowned in the roar of the radio:

The Radio

"Sails in the breath of the wind
That was all that the mind
Kept of the day; silence and scent of the pine.
Easily they will cover the wound that is mine
The wound that they made when they left me behind
The sailor, the wagtail, the bullhead, the flycatcher too.
O woman insensitive, you
Hear of the death of the wind.

The golden barrel is done
And a rag is what was the sun,
A rag on the neck of a woman in middle age
Who coughs and who never stops coughing. What can assuage
Her grief for the summer that journeyed and left her behind,
For the gold on the shoulders and gold in the pit of the thighs?
O woman deprived of your eyes,
Hear me, the singer is blind.

Night falls, shut the house fast.
Make flutes of the reeds of the past.
Open the window no more, however much they
Knock at the pane. They shout but have nothing to say.
Bring cyclamen, bring needles of pine and grasses,

ON THE GREEK STYLE

Lilies out of the sand and anemones out of the sea.
O woman, mindless, hear me,
The water's funeral passes. . . .

— Athens, the situation rapidly
Deteriorates. The public are alarmed.
The Minister declared: "No time is left. . . .
Bring cyclamen and bring the pine needles. . . .
And lilies from the sand . . . the pine needles. . . .
O woman. . . . There is an immense disparity.
The War — "

ARES DEALER IN SOULS

III

The Wreck of the Thrush

"This wood which used to bring refreshment to my
  brow
In times when midday sun put fire into the veins,
In foreign hands will blossom. Take it. I give it to you.
Look, the wood is of a lemon tree. . . ."

                                        I heard the voice
When staring into the sea I tried to distinguish
A ship which many years ago they had sunk there.
The ship's name was the *Thrush*, a small wreck, and
  the masts
Broken, groped to the bottom oblique, like tentacles,
Or memory of dreams, indicating the hull,
An indistinguishable mouth of some sea creature,
  dead,
Quenched in the water. There was total calm around.

And little by little other voices in their turn
Followed in whisperings; they were thin and thirsty

THE THRUSH

And came from the other side of the sun, the dark side;
You would say they sought to drink blood, just a drop of it.
Familiar voices but I could not recognize them.
And then there came that old man's voice, this one I felt
Drop to the heart of the day
Calm, changeless, still:
"If you sentence me to drink poison, I thank you.
Your law shall be made my law. And where should I go
Running about in foreign lands, a rolling stone?
I choose death rather.
Which of us goes to the better fate God knows."
Lands of sun, where you cannot face the sun.
Lands of man, where you cannot face the man.

As the years pass
So increase in number the judges who condemn you.
As the years pass and you speak with fewer voices,
You look with other eyes upon the sun.
You know that those who remained were cheating you;
Flesh's delirium, the lovely dance
That ends in nakedness.
As when, at night, turning into an empty highway
You suddenly see an animal's shining eyes
Which have already gone, so you feel your own eyes;
You stare at the sun, and then you are lost in the dark.
The doric chiton
Your fingers touched and it bent like the mountains
Is a marble image in light, but its head is in darkness.
And those who left the palaestra to take their bows
And shot the marathon runner full of the will to win;

ON THE GREEK STYLE

And he saw the laps of the track sailing in blood,
The world grow empty like the waning moon,
Victorious gardens withering away;
You see them in the sun, behind the sun.
And the boys who were doing diving from the bowsprits
Go down like spindles, spinning round and round,
Bare bodies plunging into the black light,
With a coin between the teeth, still swimming on,
As the sun picks out with golden needlework
Sails, wet wood and colors of the deep sea;
Even now they go down obliquely
Down to the stones of the deep,
White shining jars.

Angelic and black light,
Laughter of waves on highways of the sea,
Laughter between the tears,
The old man in supplication looks on you
As he makes his way over invisible folds,
Light mirrored in his blood
From which sprang Eteokles and Polynikes.
Angelic and black day;
The brackish taste of woman that poisons the captive
Springs from the wave, fresh sprig with sea drops on it;
O sing, little Antigone, sing O sing. . . .
I do not speak of the past, I speak of love;
Crown your hair with thorns of the sun, dark girl.
The heart of the Scorpion has set,
The tyrant inside man has gone,
And all the daughters of the deep,
Nereids, Graiae
Run to the dazzle of the springs of light.

THE THRUSH

He who has never loved shall love, in the light.
                            And you find yourself
In a great house with many windows open
Running from room to room, not knowing where first
    to look out.
Because the pines will go, and the mirrored mountains
And the chirping of birds.
The sea will empty, shattered glass, from north and
    south.
Your eyes will be emptied of the light of the day
As suddenly, of one accord, all the cicadas cease.

VIII

Cavafy and Eliot—
A Comparison

I AM not going to suggest that Constantine Cavafy and Thomas Eliot are bound together by any bonds of influence. They are too widely separated by the years — almost a whole generation. Cavafy was born in Alexandria in 1863; Eliot in St. Louis in 1888. When Eliot is still at the starting point of his orientation — about 1920, with his "Gerontion," I believe — Cavafy has already published the poems which reveal his basic characteristics.*

To be more precise, I do not mean that the Cavafy of this period is already his full self. On the contrary, with Cavafy something very extraordinary happens. In the poems of his youth and even certain poems of his middle age he quite often appears ordinary and lacking in any great distinction. But in the poems of his old age he gives the impression that he is constantly discovering things that are new and very valuable. He is "a poet of old age." A few months before his death, when he was ill in Athens, he is reported to have said, "I still have

---

The greater part of this essay was given in the form of a lecture at the British Institute, Athens, on December 17, 1946.

* I am indebted to Mr. G. P. Savides for showing me that T. S. Eliot was not unknown to Cavafy. This appears from two letters (August 1, 1924 and October 15, 1929) written by Cavafy to E. M. Forster.

twenty-five poems to write." It is sad that he was not able to write even two, even just one, of these poems. It is a strange and rare thing: he died at seventy, but he left us with the bitter curiosity we feel about a man who has been lost to us in the prime of life. But it is impossible to maintain that Cavafy was at all influenced by Eliot, even during this last period, from 1920 to 1933. As I said, Cavafy is always discovering things, but his discoveries are made only along that lonely path which he follows himself. So far as my own knowledge of literature goes, I know of no other poetry so isolated as his. From many aspects — and this is one of them — he appears as a boundary mark or limit. He remains outside the great thoroughfare that was opened to us by Solomos, and at the same time he appears to have no connection whatsoever with any European figure of his own generation or before his time. There is, I mean, no close affinity which affects his work organically. The only thing I observe here is that Cavafy has certainly breathed the atmosphere of contemporary European poetry as it was when he was between twenty and thirty-five years of age. That is, the atmosphere of the school of Symbolism from which have sprung the most important and the most dissimilar figures in prewar poetry. But he does not show the influence of any one specific writer; the marks of this school which he retains are merely the general characteristics of his generation and they soon fade away or, as his work progresses and his first attempts are left behind, take on a completely personal and individual tone.

Now to look at Eliot — the first point to notice is that the two poets are separated by the barrier of language. Our poetry keeps alive a language that is glorious and was once ecumenical; if we survey it from its heights, it deserves our attention and it is worthy of itself; and yet it cannot communicate with European literature. In between there is a great gulf fixed, the gulf of language. The rarest thing in the world is a foreign man of letters (I mean man of letters, not scholar) who knows Greek. Then too, according to the general view of foreigners, and no doubt of many Greeks too, classical Greece, Byzantine Greece and modern Greece are disconnected and independent countries; and everyone confines himself to his special subject. It is not till about the time of the beginning of the last war that we begin to observe the formation of a rather hazy consciousness that Greece is indeed a whole and that we find young people from foreign countries becoming interested in Greek poetry, not as some kind of study in linguistics but as a living art which is part of a living tradition.

So I think it very unlikely that Eliot could have been influenced by Cavafy; and in any case the question of influence does not seem to me important. What does interest me is the fact that one can, I think, legitimately speak about a parallel between the works of these poets, a parallel like the ones Plutarch wrote about — between, for instance Demetrius Poliorketes and Marc Antony, two perfectly different people; or, even better, as we speak in navigation of places which are on the same parallel and have the same climate, although they are on separate points of the globe.

Before I continue, I should like to point out the following:

(1) In speaking of Eliot's poetry I shall take most of my examples from "The Waste Land," which is, apart altogether from its value and its meaning as a symbol in modern literature, the most lapidary expression of the poet's critical ideas.

(2) I shall try to see how these critical ideas of Eliot apply to the work of Cavafy and how Cavafy stands up to these ideas. Here there is a difficulty; for while Eliot is not only the most important poet writing in English but also a distinguished essayist, critic and lecturer, Cavafy, all through his life, wrote nothing except poetry. The critical maxims which he has left us are negligible, and even these we owe to notes made by his friends — or ex-friends — which should be read with great care and circumspection. So, while we know very well the ideas and the poetics of Eliot, we can only learn the ideas and poetics of Cavafy by listening very carefully to his poetry. We all call Cavafy an Alexandrian. The epithet, I think, could do with further definition. In my view, if there is any Alexandrian ele-

ment in Cavafy it is this one: he resembles that old man of the Alexandrian sea who was constantly eluding the grasp, always changing his shape — the Proteus of Homer. . . .

"Nor was the old man forgetful of his skill in deception. . . ." For this reason we should not only guard against our inclination to be swept away by the things which we like, but should also beware of taking at their face value the superficial meaning of the words of Cavafy or of his dialectical subterfuges.

(3) My own view is that from a certain point onward — and I should place this point at about 1910 — the work of Cavafy should be read and judged not as a series of separate poems, but as one and the same poem, a "work in progress" as James Joyce would have said, which is only terminated by death. Cavafy is, I think, the most "difficult" poet of contemporary Greece, and we shall understand him more easily if we read him with the feeling of the continuous presence of his work as a whole. This unity is his grace, and it is in this way that I shall approach him.

2

THE poem of Cavafy that first made me think of Eliot was "Those Who Fought for the Achaean League":

> Valiant are you who fought and fell in glory;
> fearless of those who were everywhere victorious.

ON THE GREEK STYLE

> If Diaios and Critolaus were at fault, you are blameless.
> When the Greeks want to boast,
> "Our nation turns out such men as these," they will say
> of you. So marvelous will be your praise —
>
> Written in Alexandria by an Achaean;
> In the seventh year of Ptolemy Lathyrus.

— A brilliant epigram. The first six lines have something of the metal of Simonides:

> These on their own dear country conferred unquenchable glory,
> Taking upon themselves the darkening cloud of death.

They made me reflect upon the remarkable unity of the Greek Anthology, which, as has been observed, contains poems written over a period of about a thousand years and yet forms a whole, the newer poems merely adding something of their own to the procession of the older ones. And so, I thought, after a chasm of so many years, here comes Cavafy to add his stone to the great building. My reaction was coldly literary. I was not interested in Cavafy at that time, or not particularly. My judgment, like that of most readers, passed over the last two lines in silence. What was the point of this tailpiece which merely seemed to get in the way?

> Written in Alexandria by an Achaean,
> In the seventh year of Ptolemy Lathyrus.

CAVAFY AND ELIOT — A COMPARISON

Years passed. One night in blacked-out Alexandria, a few days after the battle of Crete, I remembered the Achaean's epigram. It was tragically actual. Perhaps because of this, perhaps because I was in the city of the Ptolemies, I whispered over the whole poem to myself, together with its final cryptic lines. And then, suddenly and for the first time, I appreciated that the poem was written in 1922, on the eve of the catastrophe in Asia Minor;* and almost without thinking I reread these lines as:

> Written in Alexandria by an Achaean,
> The year that our race was destroyed.

Now it was no longer Cavafy leaping across a chasm of the ages to take his own place in the Greek Anthology; no longer a painter of cold, casual and Parnassian portraits; here instead was a contemporary of mine and one who had found the way to express his feelings with the greatest possible brevity and lucidity, one who was able to summon Simonides and the brilliant epitaphs of ancient days to leave their broken tombs and to come to me. It was a living presence, the presence that is felt too in the lines of Solomos on the destruction of the island of Psara.

This is my example. Let us use it to try to discover, even in a limited way, what Cavafy feels about time.

* In the edition of 1926 Cavafy was careful to indicate, "First Printing: February 2, 1922."

The first date given to us by the poem is that of the year when the Achaeans fell at Leucopetra, fighting the "everywhere victorious" Romans, who now abolish all traces of Greek independence. The year is 146 B.C. In Cavafy's poetry this date has a firm connection with two other previous events which he mentions elsewhere and which were disastrous for Hellenism. One of these events is the battle of Magnesia (190 B.C.), in which the Seleucid Antiochus the Great was utterly defeated by Scipio; and the other is the battle of Pydna (168 B.C.), in which Aemilius Paulus defeated the Macedonians and made an end of their power forever. This historical moment, about fifty years in length, is in the mind of the anonymous Achaean when he envisages the beautiful dead "as something holy which you approach in adoration," and when he whispers: "If Diaios and Critolaus were at fault, you are blameless."

The last generals of the Achaean League, Diaios and Critolaus, were undoubtedly at fault. The historian Paparrigopoulos in describing their behavior calls them "peddlars" of Hellenism, of mob rule and of facts. And Polybius notes that the saying "If we are not lost soon, we can never be saved" was on everybody's lips at this time.

The tree was rotten and had to be felled. The whole period is sick:

>   . . . Now desperation and grief.
>   The boys in Rome were right.

> It is not possible for the dynasties to endure
> that came out of the Macedonian Occupation.
> [*Of Demetrius Soter*]

So speaks a disenchanted Seleucid, Demetrius, who bears a very close resemblance to this Achaean of ours. The vices which brought down in ruin the structure raised by Alexander were just as powerful as were the virtues themselves of the great Macedonian: perfidy, partiality, betrayal, political ineptitude, cunning, selfishness, bursts of temper alternating with servility. Here is Ptolemy going to Rome to ask for help against his brother:

> Poorly dressed, humble, he entered Rome,
> and lodged at the house of a little artisan.
> And there he presented himself to the Senate
> as a woebegone creature and as a pauper
> so that he might beg with greater success.
> [*The Displeasures of the Son of Seleucus*]

Or Philip V of Macedon, when he hears of the disaster at Magnesia in which his onetime ally, King Antiochus of Syria, was destroyed:

> Philip, of course, will not postpone the feast.
> However long his life's tedium has lasted,
> one good thing he retains, his memory shows no lapse.
> He recalls how much they wept in Syria, what sort of sorrow
> they felt, when their Mother Macedonia became dirt. . . .
> [*The Battle of Magnesia*]

ON THE GREEK STYLE

Finally (and many other examples could be quoted) there is the occasion when the "young man of Antioch," who has just the same tone of voice as the Achaean of the epigram, speaks to another king of Syria about the impending battle of Pydna. The young man speaks emotionally and impatiently; and the illustrious Antiochus, tongue-tied and timorous, looks round to see whether there is some eavesdropper in the background.

It is this atmosphere which is emotionally identified by the poet with the atmosphere of 1922, just before "the destruction of the race." And we know the frenetic insistence of Cavafy on his idea of "the race." "I am not a Greek," he said, "I am a Hellene."

How does Cavafy bring these two periods together? He does it by introducing a connecting link, a third intermediary date, the seventh year (the last but one) of Ptolemy VIII, Lathyrus, 109 B.C. This also was a troubled period, a period of humiliation, decadence and never-ending intrigue, which culminated in the flight of Ptolemy from Alexandria, while omnipotent Rome is all the time drawing its web closer round the pitiful kingdom of the Lagids. This is the "present time" of the poet as he writes his epigram; and the writer of the epigram, in this seventh year of any Ptolemy Lathyrus, is Cavafy, is the nameless Achaean, is both of them together.

I hope you will forgive me for this somewhat

scholastic excursion of mine. I shall go no further with it. There are some poets who write with accuracy and there are others who have no use for this quality. They are both right, though it must be admitted that those who belong to the second category are much easier to handle both for the critic and for the reader. However, though I could extend this inquiry further into other parts of Cavafy's work, I prefer to stop here for the time being. All I ask my reader to remember is this: that by alluding, almost imperceptibly, to the fault of Diaios and Critolaus and then to the seventh year of Ptolemy Lathyrus, Cavafy is able to identify the past with the present in a simultaneous moment. And this is a very different thing from the use of history which we normally find in the works of other poets, whether Romantic or Parnassian. It is no visual reminiscence, no reference to a vague mythology, no thematic treatment by the artist of "the beautiful" as seen in an icy and solitary piece of sculpture. Diaios, Critolaus, Philip, Demetrius, Ptolemy Lathyrus, the Achaean, are inside us, and inside us now; each of them could be you and I and everybody who has some consciousness of the evil and of the calamity.

> And do not rely on the fact that in your life,
> circumscribed, regulated and prosaic,
> there are no such spectacular and terrifying things.
> Perhaps at this very hour, Theodotus is entering
> the well-appointed house of one of your neighbors —

invisible, bodiless —
carrying such a hideous head.

[*Theodotus*]

This is Cavafy whispering into our ear, very softly, very insistently; it is the dreadful head of Pompey, symbol of everyday horror, here, in the middle of our tidy way of life.

This is the mirror that the poet holds up to us. In it can be reflected those who are not "contented," those who have the courage to look into it. It is the mirror of time; it is the feeling of time. To put it more simply — there is a feeling of temporal identification; past and present are united and with them, perhaps, the future as well. As Eliot says in one of his major poems:

> Time present and time past
> are both perhaps present in time future
> and time future contained in time past.

"The Waste Land" of Eliot was written in 1922, between the end of the First World War and the beginning of the years preceding the next war. To simplify a great deal, it can be described as an epic of the decline of the world in which we are still living. It is founded on an archetypal myth, on the very ancient symbols of the changes in vegetation, of germination, of fertility; on the myth of the god who rises from the dead — Adonis, Attis, Osiris, Thammuz, Christ. The fertile element is water, the sterile element is dryness, and the purifying element is fire. "The Waste Land" is a present situation between hell and purgatory; the place of the drama is a contemporary big city, London, which is identified with other famous cities either in the past or present: Jerusalem, Athens, Alexandria, Vienna. The more specific symbols employed are those of a medieval legend from the cycle of the Holy Grail. There is the figure of the "Fisher-King," whose physical decay extends to the whole of his kingdom, which has become a dried-up "Waste Land" where water does not flow, love is sterile, crops fail, and the animals do not reproduce — a condition that cannot change until the "pure Knight" brings from "the chapel perilous" the lance and the cup, the Holy Grail containing the ever-fresh blood of the Savior. If the Knight succeeds in his quest, rain will fall again, the waters will flow and fertility will return to the land. In Eliot's poem all the women represent love that is sterile, and all the men represent the dead god, except for one figure, Tiresias who "sees the essence of the poem," who thus indeed represents the poet himself. It is in his person that the male and female principles are united.

Let us now look at a passage from the first part of the poem; it describes an encounter between the poet (or Tiresias) and "one I knew" in the city of London early in the morning.

    Unreal City,
  Under the brown fog of a winter dawn,

ON THE GREEK STYLE

> A crowd flowed over London Bridge, so many,
> I had not thought death had undone so many.
> Sighs, short and infrequent, were exhaled,
> And each man fixed his eyes before his feet.
> Flowed up the hill and down King William Street,
> To where Saint Mary Woolnoth kept the hours
> With a dead sound on the final stroke of nine.
> There I saw one I knew, and stopped him, crying:
>   "Stetson!
> "You who were with me in the ships at Mylae!
> "That corpse you planted last year in your garden,
> "Has it begun to sprout? Will it bloom this year?
> "Or has the sudden frost disturbed its bed?
> "Oh keep the Dog far hence, that's friend to men,
> "Or with his nails he'll dig it up again!
> "You! hyprocrite lecteur! — mon semblable, — mon
>   frère!"

At the first reading these verses will seem much more cryptographical than Cavafy's verses on Ptolemy Lathyrus.

Apart from the untranslated verse from Baudelaire at the end, which strikes our hearing immediately, there are three other literary quotations; another one from Baudelaire, one from Dante, one from Webster's *The White Devil*; and there is a historical reference to the place name Mylae. Of course in approaching Eliot a wide factual knowledge is necessary. But, so as to avoid being distracted by details, let us examine just this historical reference.

> There I saw one I knew, and stopped him, crying:
>   "Stetson!

"You who were with me in the ships at Mylae!
"That corpse you planted last year in your garden,
"Has it begun to sprout?"

Of course here we are dealing with the myth of the dead god. The corpse is the dead god, and the question is "Will it bloom this year?" It is the agonizing question of an inhabitant of the "Waste Land": are we to see a Resurrection? So far, everything is clear. But who is this Stetson, whom we meet in a busy city street in London? He was, the poet (or Tiresias) tells us, once with him at Mylae — on the occasion of the destruction of the Carthaginian fleet in 260 B.C. And we shall meet him again in the third part of the poem under the name of

Mr. Eugenides, the Smyrna merchant
Unshaven, with a pocket full of currants
C.i.f. London.

and then again in Part IV:

Phlebas the Phoenician, a fortnight dead,
Forgot the cry of gulls, and the deep sea swell
And the profit and loss.
                    A current under sea
Picked his bones in whispers. As he rose and fell
He passed the stages of his age and youth
Entering the whirlpool.
                      Gentile or Jew
O you who turn the wheel and look to windward,
Consider Phlebas, who was once handsome and tall as
   you.

And in the hearing of the sensitive reader the note will be picked up and continued as "You! hypocrite lecteur! — mon semblable, — mon frère!"

I have tried to isolate, in as few words as possible, the main leitmotiv of the poem, that of the dead god. And all the inhabitants of the "Waste Land" are, in their own way, identified with the dead god and Phlebas the Carthaginian, Stetson, Mr. Eugenides and the others whom I have not mentioned, as You! hypocrite reader! — my fellow man — my brother!

It was this, just now, that Cavafy was telling us. He was telling us not to be self-satisfied, not to fool ourselves with the belief that our life, our tidy and calculated life, is somehow out of reach of the spectacular and of the terrible. We are all inhabitants of the "waste land" — you and I and everybody who has some consciousness of evil and of catastrophe. The dead god is no forgotten fairy tale but rather something deep inside us, something identified with this very present moment, with ourselves. And, in poetry, Eliot arrives at this point by the use of that very same feeling for historical time which we have observed in Cavafy.

This way of using time, so important in the work of both poets, is already underlined by Eliot in the observations which he makes on James Joyce's *Ulysses*. "In using the myth, in manipulating a continuous parallel between contemporaneity and antiquity, Mr. Joyce is pursuing a method which others must pursue after him. They will not be imitators any more than the scientist who uses the discoveries of an Einstein in pursuing his own, independent, further investigations. It is simply a way of controlling, of ordering, of giving a shape and a significance to the immense panorama of futility and anarchy which is contemporary history. It is a method already adumbrated by Mr. Yeats, and of the need for which I believe Mr. Yeats to have been the first contemporary to be conscious."

I think that I can legitimately maintain that this method is not only adumbrated, but is systematically employed by Cavafy long before the appearance of *Ulysses* and Joyce, and long before Yeats also.

"I am a historical poet," Cavafy said towards the end of his life. "I could never write a novel or a play; but I hear inside me a hundred and twenty-five voices telling me that I could write history."

Like most fragments of ordinary conversation, this phrase has no very precise meaning. However, I think that "historical poet" does not mean a poet who is also a historian. If the word "poet" has any meaning at all, it must mean a man who has this kind of feeling for history, this historical perception, which we have been examining in this essay.

3

WE will look rather more closely at this phrase of Cavafy's later. Just now I should like to comment upon certain criticisms which have been made on the lines I have already quoted. These criticisms concern, and eventually condemn, the use of so much learning, so many historical and other references in the composition of a poem. As for Eliot, this subject has been dealt with thoroughly already. In considering Cavafy I shall use as a starting point the opinions of some literary critics who have no sympathy at all for his method. That most industrious of all commentators on Cavafy's life and work, Mr. Timos Malanos, observes: "He introduces into his verse phrases borrowed from elsewhere, even untranslated quotations of whole passages from ancient texts, thus behaving not like a poet, but like the writer of an academic paper."

And in order to show us how bad this habit of Cavafy's is, he takes some passages from the old lexicon known as Suidas and uses them to parody Cavafy's style. The point could be a just one. Cavafy might be a Suidas in verse, just as Eliot might be a Sir James Frazer in verse, were it not for the sensibility with which each of these poets is endowed. It is through his sensibility that the poet is recognized. Intellect, learning, logical acuteness are for him very important things, but sensibility is the cornerstone for everything. As Eliot says in another context, "It is the sensuous contribution to the intelligence that makes the difference."

This is the important thing. And there is, I think, very definitely a common characteristic in the sensibilities of Eliot and of Cavafy. Eliot notes and emphasizes this point in the work of the poets of the late Elizabethan period, of the metaphysical poets and of his contemporaries: "There is a direct sensuous apprehension of thought, or a re-creation of thought into feeling." He is constantly pointing out that in all major poets of the time of Donne there was no dichotomy between the experience of life and the experience of learning, that what these poets derived from books — from Plutarch, Seneca, Montaigne — and what they derived from their own personal lives are not kept separate, but are pulsating together in the same living bloodstream.

It is just the same with Cavafy. We have only to think of one of his best known poems, "The God Abandons Antony," and Plutarch; of "Demetrius Soter" and Polybius; of "If Dead Indeed" and Eusebius. His mind hears the beloved voices in his thought. His "art of poetry" amounts to: "Attempts to numb the pain, in Imagination and Word."

I should, I think, emphasize the use of the words "mind," "thought," "word" in their reference to what is pure emotion. The poem "Caesarion" is a fine example of how for Cavafy thinking is feeling; and "Caesarion" comes into existence through "a small and trivial passage" in an obscure work of history.

"It is probable," Eliot writes, "that men ripen best through experiences which are at once sensuous and intellectual; certainly many men will admit that their keenest ideas have come to them with the quality of a sense perception, and that their keenest sensuous experience has been as if the body thought."

I think that it would be difficult to deny that here we have just the same type of sensibility as that which we find in Cavafy — a blending, an indissoluble mixture of feeling, learning and thinking. This is the basic characteristic of unity in his work, and it is just this that is missing in Suidas.

"Two poems of mine were shipwrecked because I could not find a copy of Gregory Nazianzen," Cavafy used to say to his friends. And why not? The question is not what sort of books a poet reads, but whether he can bring about a transfusion of himself into the material from which he is going to make his poems. And this is something that can be observed, not in his method, but only in his actual work. There is a remark of Rémy de Gourmont which, I should imagine, must have meant much to Eliot: "Flaubert incorporated all his sensitivity in his work. Apart from his books, he is of very little interest." This phrase should be applied in its entirety to Cavafy, if we want to understand him. In a life span of seventy years he did nothing else but distill himself, drop by drop, into his hundred and fifty or so poems:

> Environment of house, of city centers, city quarters,
> Which I look upon and where I walk; year after year

CAVAFY AND ELIOT — A COMPARISON

> I have created you in the midst of joy and in the midst of sorrows:
> With so many circumstances, so many things.
>
> And you have been made into sensation, the whole of you, for me.
>
> *[In the Same Space]*

"The craftsman, since he puts his work before everything else, must destroy himself for the sake of his work" — so Cavafy used to say, according to one of his critics. There are two ways in which we can examine the personal life of an artist: one is by means of anecdotes, surprises, jokes, medical reports; the other is by humbly trying to see how the poet incorporates his perishable life in his work. For those who prefer the first way, my words may have very little significance; I prefer the second, and this is why I say that Cavafy, apart from his poetry, has no great interest.

But, one may ask, if Cavafy is incorporating his sensibility in his poetry, why is he so arid? Why does his verse not have, as some have complained, "the ring of a hymn, why does it not sing, why does it not throb with passion? Why is it a versification of the intellect?" And it is perfectly true that Cavafy does not sing and does not throb with passion; he seems indeed fully conscious of his idiosyncrasy, which is, as we have seen, to think with the senses. His critics go on to say, "Cavafy's method is always to use the most frugal and anti-poetic phrase for the expression of his poetic ideas." He is "the implacable enemy of any kind of decoration." And, worst of all, "With the passing of the years he became accustomed to a facile and continuous increase in the use of the prosaic element," like "one who, always a heavy drinker, has continually to increase the daily dose."

There is no doubt of the fact that "Cavafy stands at the boundary where poetry strips herself in order" (as I have said elsewhere) "to become prose." No one has ever gone further in this direction. He is the most anti-poetic (or a-poetic) poet I know — if, that is, one measures and defines the poetic by the aims and the work of Solomos. Naturally, if we look at things in this way, we shall have to arrive in the end at the conclusion that "Cavafy betrayed poetry."

However, it is very dangerous to use one poet for measuring another. If we like Solomos (and I am devoted to him) we should look for him in his own work and in the work of those whom he helped to express themselves. Not where he does not exist. And in Cavafy Solomos does not exist. Cavafy belongs to an entirely different Greek tradition — a colossal tradition and one that is much more arrogant than that other one, the one that was looked down upon and which Solomos tried to grab hold of with both his hands, which failed him in the task. Cavafy's tradition, the scholarly tradition, rests upon a tremendous weight of literature; however, in all its thousand years of existence (if we put aside the church hymns) it has not been able to produce poetry like that of Solomos, and, like Cavafy, it has not been able to communicate feelings.

Cavafy has this tradition in the very marrow of his bones, so deeply that although in his early work he tried to shake it off, he still kept it, and ended by trying to put life into it by the transfusion of his own blood. We have, of course, to shape our material; but at the same time our material shapes us. Cavafy's material is dry, prosaic, sentimentally neutral, abstract. In these respects it is the exact opposite of the material used by Solomos. Solomos and Cavafy follow courses which lead in opposite directions; they start from antipodes; they *are* the antipodes that form the limits of the immense horizon in the literary landscape of our small country. The material of Solomos is bursting with life, untamed, full of color, vigor, instinct; and with this material he struggles incessantly with the knowledge, the sagacity and the discipline of a great European; he struggles to bring it under the control of the exactitude and order of a higher form of expression. Cavafy, on the other hand, is dealing with a material that has grown old in monasteries and libraries, and he tries to incarnate through his own body (let us not laugh at him; perhaps Lysias the Grammarian is his most pathetic character) this matter which is as wholly devoid of feeling as is the empty shell of a cicada, but which conserves the wisdom and the old technique of the movement of speech and of accuracy. These are the two diametrically opposite ways followed by Solomos and by Cavafy. However, earth is a sphere, and perhaps they have already met.

The only things, then, which this tradition brought to Cavafy were abstract motions and the forms of accuracy. It was a choreography without a dancer; the dancer must be provided by Cavafy himself. His tradition, to which he had to remain true, provided him with no material for hymns, songs, heartthrobs. It was — if one wants to look at it in this way — full of exclamations, but these exclamations were all hollow, sounds and noises with no human voice behind them. Working in this tradition and with his own idiosyncrasy, Cavafy could not possibly force exclamations from his lips, he could not possibly be lyrical. But there are other forms in which poetry can exist — in the expression of human activity, for instance. "What great poetry is not dramatic?" Eliot asks. "Even the minor writers of the Greek Anthology, even Martial, are dramatic. Who is more dramatic than Homer or Dante? We are human beings and in what are we more interested than in human action and human attitudes?"*

In this sense of "dramatic" (the reader has, perhaps, noted the mention of the Greek Anthology)

* *A Dialogue on Dramatic Poetry.*

Cavafy too is dramatic. In another essay* Eliot writes, "The only way of expressing emotion in the form of art is by finding an 'objective correlative'; in other words, a set of objects, a situation, a chain of events, which shall be the formula of that *particular* emotion; such that when the external facts, which must terminate in sensory experience, are given, the emotion is immediately invoked."

This "objective correlative" of Eliot can lead us far. Let us see how it can be applied to Cavafy. What Eliot is saying I imagine, is that in order to be able to express his emotion the poet has to find a setting of situations, a framework of events, a form-type, which will be like the sights of a rifle; when the senses are 'sighted' in this way they will find themselves directed at the particular emotion. The framework of events in the *Odyssey*, the *Divine Comedy*, or *Antony and Cleopatra*, for example (and I mean not only the plot of these works, but also, and mainly, the psychology and pattern of behavior of their characters) is the "objective correlative" of the special emotion which Homer, Dante, or Shakespeare wish to express; the objective correlative is a tool of accuracy.

Cavafy seems to be constantly using this method; and as the years pass, he seems to reject altogether the unframed expression of emotion. He goes even further; he not only insists on the agility of his characters, the lapidary quality of his events, and

* *Hamlet.*

the clarity of his historical perceptions which form his own "objective correlative," but he also seems to erase, to neutralize, all other kinds of emotive expression either by the robustness of the language or by the use of other poetic modes, imageries, comparisons or transpositions. This is another reason why Cavafy has been called graceless and prosaic.

Very often in Cavafy's work, while the language itself is neutral and unemotional, the movement of the persons and the succession of the events involved is so closely packed, so airtight, one might almost say, that one has the impression that his poems breathe emotion through a vacuum. This vacuum created by Cavafy is the element which differentiates his phrases from the mere prosaicness which his critics have fancied that they saw in his work. Petros Vlastos,* who dislikes Cavafy almost as much as he dislikes Eliot, writes that his poems are "like pedestals without the statues." If one leaves out of account the implied derision, I should say that this is not a bad description. Often Cavafy's poems reveal the emotion that we should have felt at the sight of a statue which is no longer there; it was there, there where we once saw it, there in the place from which it has now been removed. But they do reveal the emotion. Maybe this "absence of the statue" is the greatest difficulty in Cavafy, but when he writes in this way I admire him more than in those early halftoned whisperings of a kind

* Essayist, critic and scholar (1879–1941).

of youthful aestheticism. Consider the following as an example of his later manner:

> Successful and entirely satisfied,
> the King Alexander Jannaeus
> and his consort the Queen Alexandra,
> preceded by a fanfare of music, pass with
> all kinds of splendor and luxury
> through the streets of Jerusalem.
> The work undertaken by Judas Maccabaeus
> and his four illustrious brothers,
> and continued later with such dogged resolve,
> amid perils and many difficulties,
> has succeeded magnificently.
> Now nothing inappropriate remains.
> All submission to the arrogant monarchs
> of Antioch has ceased. Look,
> the King Alexander Jannaeus
> and his consort the Queen Alexandra
> are equal in all to the Seleucids.
> Good Jews, pure Jews, faithful Jews — above all.
> But, as circumstances require it,
> they are also masters of the Greek vernacular;
> and they associate with Greeks and hellenized
> monarchs — as equals, however, and that goes without
> saying.
> The work undertaken by the great Judas Maccabaeus
> and his four illustrious brothers
> has truly succeeded magnificently,
> has succeeded remarkably.
>   [*Alexander Jannaeus and Alexandra*]

This is the pedestal: a king and his queen "successful," "entirely satisfied," conscious of their power and rank, loyal to their race and creed, proud of having continued the work of their ancestors. Their state is secure; the beautiful procession now going through the streets of Jerusalem is an impressive symbol of sovereignty. Everything is successful, healthy, prosperous. Now, what is the statue that is missing?

In another of his poems Cavafy depicts Nero, sleeping in his palace, unconscious, quiet, happy, prosperous, while his Lares (his domestic gods), terror-struck, listen to the oncoming footsteps of the avenging Erinyes. Should we not ask ourselves whether, in this poem too, there may be Lares listening to such iron footsteps? Whether, perhaps, the poet expects us, the readers, to be the Lares and to hear the Erinyes? Cavafy has told us: "Seldom, if ever, do I make use of emphasis." When we do encounter it, it should certainly mean something. It did not come there by chance or through a kind of lyrical transport.

Now it is easy to see where the emphasis is in this poem. We have only to look at the repetitions. They highlight two points: the race of Judah and the struggle of the Maccabees to make their country free and independent. These two points mark the deception, for what is happening is just the opposite.

The conquest, the great Diaspora, the persecution, the endless agony of the Jews are there, muttering in their sleep, as if dreaming of Alexander Jannaeus and of his Queen and of the great Judas Maccabaeus and his four illustrious brothers, all of whom will dissolve just like dreams as soon as, in a very few years, Destruction awakes. The missing statue is Destruction.

People have spoken of the humor of Cavafy. I think that what humor he has may be something he retained from his early childhood, when, we are told, until he reached the age of nine the only language he spoke was English. It is that type of humor — the least comprehensible element in the English language — which is expressed by the untranslatable word "nonsense," as we find it in Lewis Carroll and Edward Lear — an impassive, cold sort of jocularity, which sounds idiotic to clever people, something that creates an intellectual vacuum. For instance, Lewis Carroll's Alice talks in a wood with two strange and toylike figures. They point out to her the Red King asleep under a tree: "He's dreaming now," said Tweedledee, "and what do you think he's dreaming about?" — Alice said, "Nobody can guess that." — "Why, about *you*!" Tweedledee exclaimed. . . . "And if he left off dreaming about you, where do you suppose you'd be?" — "Where I am, of course," said Alice. — "Not you! . . . You'd be nowhere. Why you're only a sort of thing in his dream!" — "If that there King was to wake," added Tweedledum, "you'd go out — bang! — just like a candle!"

So Cavafy's poems often give us the impression that somebody who is not exactly there, but who nevertheless exists, will very soon wake up and then everything will be overturned.

What comes after this I do not know. From this point everyone must proceed in his own way. If poetry were not deeply rooted in our bodies and in our world, it would be a short-lived thing. To stop short at this point, it would have had to be a short-lived thing. We do not know the end of poetry.

4

AND now, after this long parenthesis, let us look back at that phrase of Cavafy's: "I am a historical poet." I said that this could only mean that he is a poet with a certain kind of feeling for history. On this point Eliot has some very definite ideas. Let us consider some of the most characteristic of these.

For Eliot "the historical sense involves a perception, not only of the pastness of the past, but of its presence"; and it "compels a man to write not merely with his own generation in his bones, but with the feeling that the whole of the literature of Europe from Homer and within it the whole of the literature of his own country has a simultaneous existence and composes a simultaneous order." So far from being an indolent absorption in the tepid waters of old ways and manners, it is "what makes a writer most acutely conscious of his place in time, of his own contemporaneity."*

I do not know what Cavafy's views were about

* *Tradition and the Individual Talent.*

his own contemporary world nor about the value of man in general. But when I look at his work I cannot help observing that his poetic conscience behaves as if it were in agreement with these views which have just been expressed; his historical sense not only makes him eminently contemporary, but also provides him with just the same method. The permanent element that is endlessly stressed by Cavafy — so much so that it becomes a kind of basic code in his poems — is deception, derision. The panorama unfolded by his poems is a world of dupes and swindlers. Ever since his early years (when in a poem later suppressed he wrote, "O wretched lyre, victim of every kind of deceit"), ever since his first poems (in one of which he shows Apollo deceiving Thetis like a common scoundrel), up to the very last verse he wrote (". . . let him babble./ The important thing is that he nearly burst with rage"), his whole work presents a web of trickeries, traps, ruses, machinations, fears, suspicions, faulty reckonings, mistaken expectations, vain efforts. His gods mock, deride and jeer, his characters are deceitful and at the same time mere playthings in the hands of the gods, of time, of fate, of luck, "a bone thrown to puppies, a crust of bread in a fishpond, an ant's hardships and drudgery, scurrying of mice, puppets moved by strings."*

There is no saving faith, only a faith in art, and this serves as a kind of narcotic elixir in the general

---

* Marcus Aurelius. *Meditations 7.3.*

betrayal, where we find spun round in the dreadful vortex the noble resignation of a few elderly ladies and a bitter devotion to the great race and tradition of the Greeks. Everything is "in part . . . in part."

Cavafy's world exists in the twilight zones, in the borderlands of those places, individuals and epochs which he so painstakingly identifies. It is an area marked by blending, amalgamation, transition, alteration, exceptions; the cities that glow and flicker — Antioch, Alexandria, Sidon, Seleucia, Osroene, Commagene; a hermaphroditic world where even the language spoken is an alloy. And his much publicized eroticism either takes on the behavior of a condemned person, growing old in prison, who, with a fierce insistence, tattoos erotic scenes upon his skin, or else it is diluted among a multitude of dead people and their epitaphs. The tomb of Eurion, the tomb of the Grammarian Lysias, the tomb of Iases, the tomb of Ignatius, the tomb of Lanes; Leucios, Ammones, Myres, Marylos — and so many others. There are so many dead and they are so much alive that we are unable to distinguish them from the men we saw a minute ago, as we were walking in the street, standing at the door of the café, sitting by a casino table, or working in an ironsmith's shop. His "vain, vain love," his barren love is unable to leave anything behind except a mortuary statue, typically beautiful, a cinnamon-brown suit, frayed and discolored, tragically alive, as though fallen from time's saddlebags. This is Ca-

CAVAFY AND ELIOT — A COMPARISON

vafy's panorama. All these things together make up the experience of his sensibility — uniform, contemporary, simultaneous, expressed by his historical sense. If I did not think of him in this way, I should not be able to understand him at all; put out of this perspective, *To Antiochus Epiphanes*, for instance, would have seemed to me simply ridiculous:

The young man of Antioch said to the King,
"A beloved hope pulses in the depths of my heart;
once more the Macedonians, Antiochus Epiphanes,
the Macedonians are involved in the major struggle.

If only they would triumph — I would willingly give
anyone the lion and the horses, the Pan of coral,
and the elegant palace, and the Tyrian gardens,
and all else you have given me, Antiochus Epiphanes."
Perhaps for a brief moment the King was a little moved.
But at once he remembered his father and brother,
and he did not even reply. An eavesdropper might go
and repeat something. — Besides, as was natural,
the horrible ending came quite suddenly at Pydna.

So much for the historical sense of the old poet of Alexandria. One must own that though he has employed it among innumerable forms and though he has entrusted to death the key, he transmits to us the taste of a kind of horror. Eliot too has seen something of this horror.

ON THE GREEK STYLE

5

HOWEVER, Eliot is very different from Cavafy, in the hierarchy of his values, in his technique, in his particular use of language and in the tone of his voice. He comes from another race. Sprung from a line of puritans, he sets out from America, at that time still provincial in matters of literature, to discover the workshops of the old world. For him tradition is not a matter of inheritance; if you want it, you must work hard to acquire it. An Englishman would not feel like this. But Eliot comes from a rootless place, a place without a past. He feels strongly how paper-thin, how groundless, how unreal and anarchic is, in fact, the order offered by the mechanical civilization of today, his inheritance of material good. He is aware of the drying up of the sources of inspiration. He has given himself up, both by inclination and in accord with the tenets of his own tradition, to the examination of conscience; he audits and he evaluates. Life, for him, is not pleasure; indeed, for Eliot pleasure has something in it of sarcasm; it gives the impression of a bruised fruit, a wound in a tender body. For him the element which makes mankind alive is the struggle between good and evil. He sees a world that is losing its principle of existence, that is dying out just because this struggle is sinking down into apathetic vulgarity. From this feeling comes the symbol of "the waste land," and those going to and fro there, in the words of Dante, *fece per viltà il gran rifiuto* — they are the people who never lived, because they denied both good and evil. Refused even by Hell, they cannot pass over Acheron; they are dead and neutral to the end of time.

It is in Europe that Eliot finds his tradition, the French Symbolists and Jules Laforgue, to whom he is so much indebted; the English Elizabethans and Jacobeans, the metaphysical poets and John Donne; the Mediterranean and Dante. With his religious instinct and his conscious decision to give himself to something beyond and above himself, with an amazing concentration of his own sensibility, he goes steadily forward in the production of a work that is superbly organized. He is a rare example of a poet who feels, thinks, struggles with himself, and develops a self-disciplined, almost mystical devotion to his work.

Cavafy is something different. He comes from one of the intellectual capitals of the world which, though almost submerged, is still great and can boast of being "Greek from ages past": from Constantinople, Antioch, Alexandria, the Phanar; from the capital of an intellectual fatherland which is marked by innumerable graves, but is still immense; her frontiers are far-flung and extend deep into "Bactria, as far as the Indias"; of this immensity he is the last inhabitant. When he was twelve years old or so, he set himself the task of composing a historical dictionary. He abandoned it after writing down what was for him the fateful word — *Alexander*. The "common language of the Greeks" which he inherited and came to develop "like an eavesdropper" is the language of the great masters of Hellenism. He is their last heir.

Cavafy is not burdened by the absence of a tradition. On the contrary, what he feels is the dead weight of a tradition which is thousands of years old and which he has done nothing to acquire, since he "carries in him" this "glorious" literate tradition of the Greeks. He is the solitary of an extreme period of Hellenism, the period of the twentieth century. We may compare him with Synesius in the fifth century A.D., bishop of Ptolemais, admirer of Homer, friend of Hypatia, who was baptized on the same day as he was made bishop; or with the archbishop Michael Choniates in the twelfth century, lamenting over the ancient glories of Athens. So in this boundless country surrounded by "great and high walls" he goes forward, treading with his sensitive feet upon "faces of the dead." And the whole question is whether the graves will suck him down or whether he will be able to bring to life with his own blood even so much as a single dry twig in this dead garden — a thing that, for a thousand years before him, no one has yet done in this tradition.

This duality, or division, in Cavafy is something innate. He does not come across it as he grows; he started with it and from it. He does not try to repress it; instead he looks for a way of bringing it together as he gradually develops, "almost imperceptibly," in accordance with his own way, his inner nature, his particular sincerity. In Cavafy we shall not find the presence of a world conscience, the anguished questionings, the disciplined struggle that we observe in Eliot. The shade and color of his world, of the contemporary world, is seen by Cavafy in an intuitive way. And the symbols of his "waste land" may be found without going back to forgotten myths; they are inside him; they are himself. For in the ultimate analysis of his poetry only two symbols are left: the dead Adonis who is not restored to life — the sterile Adonis, and Proteus, old, exhausted and sick — the "Fisher-King," who can no longer take on different shapes, and who asks from the magicians of the East herbs and distilled potions to dull the pain of his wound. But in the kingdom of the Alexandrian there is no "pure Knight" to symbolize the fight between good and evil. We have seen how Eliot used the verse of Dante: *Che fece per viltà il gran rifiuto*. This same verse provided Cavafy with the opportunity (before, it is true, he had found the direction in which he was to go) of writing his most popular poem, which is also, in my view, his least successful. Perhaps it is his only poem where he does not pay attention to his words. He places in opposition, with some grandiloquence and with the use of capital letters, "the great Yes" and "the great No" — terms which here neither lead to nor start from any reality. But the problems of the puritans are very rarely problems for Greeks, and Eliot might have seemed to Cavafy just another Julian the Apostate, Julian the puritan, the most derided figure who appears in his work.

The distance separating Eliot and Cavafy is enormous. However, this Phanariot, who at the beginning appears to have no talent for poetry at all, and yet who, like a true poet, perseveres until he becomes "true to himself," gradually discarding everything that does not belong to him, gave us, in his own particular manner and perhaps unconsciously (like a natural ripening of growth), with the aid of the images of his ancestral coat of arms, his own poetical expression of "the waste land." The invocation of the resurrection of the dead god which he wrote towards the end of his life is to me one of the most beautiful passages in the Greek language:

> "What extract can be discovered from
> witching herbs," said an aesthete,
> "what extract prepared according to the
> formulas of ancient Grecosyrian magi
> that, for a day (if its potency
> can last no longer), or even an hour,
> can evoke for me my twenty-three years. . . ."
> [*According to Ancient Formulas of Greco-Syrian Magi*]

"Eliot has been criticized," I have written elsewhere, "for leaving his reader in a dry, sterile and waterless waste land, alone, and with no hope of salvation. There might be some point in this if Eliot had not created any poetry. Because poetry, however marked by despair, saves us, in some way or other, from the tumult of our passions."

I should say the same thing about Cavafy. The job of a poet is not to solve philosophical or social problems; it is to offer us poetic catharsis by means of his passions and his thoughts, which are concerned both with his inner self and with the world outside him, as is becoming to a living man with his share in this world. Cavafy, as I see him, lying stranded, as he is, in the net of the dead god, gives us this poetical catharsis out of his spiritual heritage, out of his foreknowledge of the world, out of his buried secret, and out of the logic of his personality. However, from his "waste land," as from that of Eliot, there is no exit. The problem remains, and to solve it one would have to change many things in the life of the world we live in. But that is another matter.

This ecumenical problem, in its various forms and its various reactions, goes very deep and marks very deeply the living literature of our times. It is also expressed, as I have attempted to show, by the poetry of Cavafy, Cavafy the grammarian, if we look at him, "with a searching soul," that is to say a soul which cannot but be part of the world we live in. Artemidorus also was a grammarian. But if

Caesar had read what he had written down, things would have been different:

> As you go out on the street,
> a man of authority conspicuous with your followers,
> if by some chance out of the mob some Artemidorus
> should approach you, who brings you a letter,
> and hastily says, "Read this at once,
> it contains grave matters of concern to you,"
> do not fail to stop; do not fail to put off
> all talk or work; do not fail to turn away
> the various people who salute you and kneel before you
> (you can see them later); let even the Senate
> itself wait, and immediately get to know
> the grave writings of Artemidorus.
>
> [*The Ides of March*]

The "grave writings" of Artemidorus, of Cavafy, of Eliot, of Flaubert. "If at least they had understood *Education Sentimentale*," said Flaubert, looking at the ruins of the Tuileries, in the strife-torn Paris of the Commune, "this would not have happened." Flaubert must have been a naïve man in politics. And in any case, as Gourmont said, Flaubert, who was distilling himself drop by drop into his books, is of no interest to us apart from his works. I would say the same thing of Cavafy. I said this before and now I will correct the statement by saying that outside his poems Cavafy does not exist. As it seems to me, one of two things will happen: either we shall continue to write scholastic gossip about his private life, fastening upon the bons mots of provincial witticisms; and then, of course, we shall reap what we have sown; or else, starting from his basic characteristic, his unity, we shall listen to what is actually said by his work, this work in which, drop by drop, he spent his own self, with all his senses. And after having done this, we might attempt to place him and to feel him within the framework of the Greek tradition, the whole tradition, indivisible as it is. For this tradition is not, as some see it, an affair of isolated promontories, some great names, some illuminating texts; instead it is like what others of us see and feel in the little mosaics of a humble Byzantine church — the Ionian philosophers, the popular verses of the period of the Comneni, the epigrams of the Anthology, Greek folk song, Aeschylus, Palamas, Solomos, Sikelianos, Calvos, Cavafy, the Parthenon, Homer, all living in a moment of time, in this Europe of today and looking at our devastated homes. With this point of view Cavafy will not seem to us alien; rather we shall find him slowly and mysteriously becoming one with his own kind (though not with the grammarians and the sophists), becoming more and more closely united, more and more integrated with our living tradition, like Myres, changed and confirmed by time, "dealer in souls."

IX

Letter to a Foreign Friend

My dear friend,

Circumstances have forced me to answer your letter about Eliot in an autobiographical manner. I'm sorry about this, but I happen to be here without my books and manuscripts. I am a traveler here — and that must be my excuse.

From 1932 until recent years I have often lived in the company of Eliot's poetry. Among the many debts I owe him, by no means the least outstanding is the better knowledge I acquired, through the study of his work, of the English language and literature: an important gift for one who is self-taught in these matters, as I am.

I remember the time — it now seems so long ago — when I was making my first faltering discovery of London, which I thought of as a gigantic seaport, and of the English language, whose music sounded so much more fluid than that of our own tongue. Also, the shock I experienced at the sour taste of death in the fog, and the intensified circulation of fear in the arteries of the great city. Death, I kept thinking, is for us a sudden wound; here it

---

Translated by Nanos Valaoritis and amended by Edmund Keeley. A somewhat abridged form of this essay originally appeared in England under the title *T. S. Eliot in Greece* in *T. S. Eliot: a Symposium*, compiled by Richard March and Tambimuttu (London, 1948).

is a slow poison. I carried with me a great nostalgia, which was awakened on many occasions by the kind of formless sensitivity and patient, really rather cold politeness with which I was surrounded. I had no friends in England then. My only acquaintances were the crowds in the streets and the museums. The pre-Raphaelite paintings in the Tate Gallery bored me. I often had to rush out of my house to see again a fragment of the Greek marbles — especially, for reasons I won't dwell on, the one of the Ilissus — or a small portrait by El Greco at the National Gallery. An unconfirmed idea had taken root in my mind that the model for this picture must have been a Cretan boatman.

Some days before Christmas 1931 I visited a bookshop in Oxford Street to look for some Christmas cards, and for the first time, among the colorful engravings, I took a poem by Eliot in my hands. It was "Marina" from the series of Ariel Poems.

> What seas what shores what gray rocks and what islands
> What water lapping the bow
> And scent of pine . . .

From that time onward up till the time when I first read "The Dry Salvages," one afternoon in 1941, in Cape Town, to this very day as I write to you from a high plateau surrounded by the naked steppe, this lovely bow which forges slowly ahead has impressed itself on my mind as one of the most striking features of Eliot's poetry. In case this may seem strange to you, you must bear in mind that for many of us the bows of ships have a special place in the imagery of our childhood, as perhaps do the shapes of footballs or the photos of deceased relatives for other people.

Anyhow, I went back home with "Marina" and a small volume of poems, bound in mauve material, the one that ends with "The Hollow Men," if I'm not mistaken. The proverb from Petronius Σίβυλλα τί Θέλεις made me glance at "The Waste Land." I don't think I understood much of the pattern of that poem. The inner regions of English literature, of which it assumes some knowledge, were mostly unknown to me; but the dramatic manner of expression had aroused my interest. After the outburst of dadaism and the experiments of surrealism which I had witnessed in France, after these tremendous excavations and explosions of the ego which had brought into the atmosphere at that time the sort of electrical tension one finds in tropical climates just before the advent of the rains, the renewal of the dramatic tradition which I found in Eliot brought me back to a more temperate zone. I feel it may be surprising that I talk in this way of a poem like "The Waste Land," which more than any other gives the sensation of thirst among the dry cactuses, a sensation with which we were so familiar in those happy-go-lucky days. The difference is that this thirsting despair found its expression in France in

ON THE GREEK STYLE

the search for a technique of despair, whereas in the England of Eliot it was treated less abstractly in terms of actual human character.

> "You who were with me in the ships at Mylae!
> "That corpse you planted last year in your garden,
> "Has it begun to sprout? Will it bloom this year?
> "Or has the sudden frost disturbed its bed?
> "Oh keep the Dog far hence, that's friend to men,
> "Or with his nails he'll dig it up again!
> "You! hypocrite lecteur! — mon semblable, — mon frère!"

It was a long time since I had heard such a note, and "Hieronymo's mad againe" moved me long before I had read even a line from Kyd. To put it in simpler words, apart from the image of the Mediterranean "Marina," the poetry of Eliot offered me something much deeper, something which was inevitably moving to a Greek: the elements of tragedy.

But there was also another old acquaintance of mine who made me feel a special affinity to Eliot: a Frenchman whom I came to love very much soon after arriving in Paris as a student at the end of the First World War — Jules Laforgue. Now that I look back on those years, after our recent ordeals, they seem to me part of a script for a Charlie Chaplin movie. What a plaything the *grosse Bertha* was compared to the blitz and the V–2! The humor of it could still amuse. Who was it (Apollinaire or

LETTER TO A FOREIGN FRIEND

someone else?) who said, when that fat German gun fired its first shot on Paris: "Bah! They've stepped on the Eiffel Tower's corn." It was the beginning of the Jazz Age. I was buying hazelnuts from a street vendor when I saw one of her bombs explode at the far end of an avenue. Paris was completely empty when I entered it in July; by November it was full to the point of asphyxiation with armistice celebrations. You couldn't find a hole to crawl into anywhere. My room was the iciest place I've ever known. An itinerant violinist would come around every afternoon to grate my stomach with a desperately languorous tune. In the evenings, as I crossed the bridge of Saint Michel, an old woman selling violets would wail: *"Pour vos amours, 'sieurs, 'dames."* I was reading in those days both Homer and the wildest avant-garde journals. I was marvelously lost and dreamstruck. That's when I came to know Laforgue. What first brought me close to him was, I think, my freezing student room. I would love to have at hand the book with that letter in it so that I could reread it now — a letter from Laforgue to his sister sent from a room just like mine at that time, on the rue du Sommerard, if I'm not mistaken. That young man, who was dead at the age of twenty-eight, seemed to me a brother ten years older than I was. I liked his ways. I was amazed that he was ignored or disdained in France. He was not in fashion. Rimbaud and Lautréamont had squashed him. Yet *c'était une belle âme, comme*

ON THE GREEK STYLE

on n'en fait pas aujourd'hui, as he used to say. I knew almost all of his verse by heart. As I write you now, gazing out of my window at the impersonal snow-covered horizon, any number of his landscapes intrude between the paper I'm darkening and the snow.

Honestly, I've always found strange and noteworthy the difficulty, the surprise, that important men of letters in England felt on first confronting "Prufrock." A Frenchman, Alain-Fournier for example, wouldn't have been surprised at all. At the most, he might have noticed that the young man Laforgue had introduced him to was bearing one or two more decades on his back and that he had begun to lose his hair.

I am still grateful to that unknown shopgirl who offered me the poems I mentioned instead of "Ash Wednesday." If my acquaintance with Eliot had started with that poem, I fear that this first spark of emotion, this gift of God which counts for so much in such circumstances, would have been lost forever. You see, we are a people who have had great Church Fathers, but we are now without great mystics; we are devoted to emotions and ideas, but we like to have even the most abstract notions presented in a familiar form, something which a Christian of the West would call idolatry. Also, we are — in the original sense of the word — very conservative. None of our traditions, Christian or pre-Christian, have really died out. Often when I attend the ritual procession on Good Friday, it is difficult for me to decide whether the god that is being buried is Christ or Adonis. Is it the climate? Is it the race? I can't tell. I believe it's really the light. There must surely be something about the light that makes us what we are. In Greece one is more friendly, more at one with the universe. I find this difficult to express. An idea becomes an object with surprising ease. It seems to become all but physically incarnated in the web of the sun. On the other hand, at times you cannot discern whether the mountain opposite is a stone or a gesture. The *Logos* in its disembodied form is something which transcends our powers. And horror when it falls in our country falls with mechanical exactitude. Perhaps this explains some aspects of our character which shock the foreigner; and perhaps this too may have some relation to the structure of the ancient drama. You must excuse me if I have departed from my subject. I only wanted to find a way of expressing the fact that though I have often in the past had discussions with English friends who admired "Ash Wednesday" without reservations or even thought more highly of it than of any other of Eliot's poems, my feeling remains that in these lines:

> Who walked between the violet and the violet
> Who walked between
> The various ranks of varied green

the effect is rather that of a heraldic decoration than of a sensitive image. I also feel rather guilty that I cannot respond to the following lines:

> If the lost word is lost, if the spent word is spent
> If the unheard, unspoken
> Word is unspoken, unheard . . .

The *Quartets* are far more difficult poems — though the word seldom means anything in poetry — yet they function in a very different way. That is why I sometimes think that in the case of "Ash Wednesday" one finds the same thing as that to which Eliot draws attention in Shakespeare, in *Hamlet:* a certain difficulty in his use of the "objective correlative." Yet it is more probable that the fault is mine. Poetry does not mean the same thing to all people; it does not create the same impression on everyone, and sometimes it brings the same result with different means. Take, for example, "The Waste Land." I believe that in one way or another, in a positive or negative, direct or indirect manner, the feeling "Waste Land" (let us call it this for short) runs through all the poetic expression of our times. The person who might be said to have expressed this feeling in Greece is an old man — I nearly said Gerontion — who carried, inherently, a tradition enormous in both depth and quantity. But he has no inclination to reform. On the contrary, he has an obvious loathing for any reformer. He writes as though he were telling us: "If men are such as they are, let them go where they deserve to be. It is not my business to correct them." He is a mythologist with an astonishing feeling for history — history, I mean, in Eliot's sense. One is never quite sure when one reads him whether a youth who works in a poor blacksmith's shop in contemporary Alexandria will not turn up in the evening at one of the dives where the subjects of Ptolemy Lathyrus are holding their revels, or if the favorite of Antiochus Epiphanes has not in mind to discuss with the King the outcome of Rommel's operations in Libya. Surrounded with tombs and epitaphs — it is Cavafy I am speaking of — he lives in a huge cemetery, where with torment, a mellow kind of torment, he invokes endlessly the resurrection of a young body; of an Adonis who, as the years pass, seems to change and become vilified by a love which is continually more vulgar. It seems as though the mind of the poet in his despair soaks in vitriol the dead body he cannot revive. This old man has really no sense of the Purgatory in his veins nor of Hell. He cherishes his sins. He is sorry that the decay of his old age does not allow him to commit more. His only aspiration is to remain Hellenic. "Humanity has no capacity more precious than this," he used to say. They say that on the last piece of paper he held in his hand before he died — he had by then lost his voice — he marked a dot and around it a circle, to underline it. That was all. He ended his life with a dot, in the same way as his carefully written poems. This grammarian sometimes gives the impression that he is a "mystic without a God" — if this phrase of Madame Emilie Teste's can have a certain meaning.

I mention the case of Cavafy, for it can show, approximately and with a great deal of simplification, the geographic position in which one might place Greek poetry in relation to that of Eliot. Yet, though Cavafy — in his own manner and with his own traditions, and after all the necessary distinctions have been taken into account — did write a "Waste Land," defined, that is to say, the region from which we feel so pressing a need to escape, he could never have written the *Quartets*. However, Greece, as my friend Rex Warner has remarked, though a small country, is in reality many Greeces. Cavafy represents only one of these. The poet who could, if he had not been born one hundred and fifty years ago, have come nearer to the *Quartets* is Dionysios Solomos. He, like Eliot, is an extremely sensitive reader of Dante, and, like Eliot, gifted with an extraordinary auditory imagination. He was "*Il miglior fabbro del parlar materno*" for us all, I believe, not so much for what he achieved as for what he strove to achieve. It is a remarkable trick of fate that the new Greek poetry began with him, whom we could much more easily imagine a contemporary of Mallarmé than of Byron. The precious inheritance he left us consists only of fragments of work which were never completed, and terrible blank spaces. It is an inheritance that delineates boundaries for us. In any case, the contemporary reader must experience a strange feeling when he reads in the introduction to Solomos's poems (written by his best friend, who after his death preserved all he could of his work) sentences such as these: "His art was a spontaneous and incessant effort to merge his personality in the absolute truth, applying the axiom of Heraclitus: 'There is a truth that is common to everybody, yet most people live as though they had a wisdom of their own.'" This extract, written in October 1859, will remind you, I am sure, of the phrase Eliot wrote in his essay, on "Tradition and the Individual Talent": "The progress of an artist is a continual self-sacrifice, a continual extinction of personality." The axiom of Heraclitus, on the other hand, serves as a motto to the *Four Quartets*.

This is my answer to your question on the relation of Eliot to Greek poetry, and I am afraid it is not very satisfactory. Apart from this, as far as contemporary matters are concerned, I am not much use as a witness. Incidentally, there are critics in my country who say that in the few poems I have written they discern the influence of Eliot. This does not surprise me, for I believe that there is no parthenogenesis in art. Each one of us is made up of a number of things, and the lion too *"est fait de mouton assimilé,"* wrote Paul Valéry. Precisely, for it is the assimilation that matters — but it is very difficult to discuss such an obscure process. The fact is I attempted to translate "The Waste Land" into Greek, as well as some other poems of Eliot's. I did this for two reasons: first, because I had no other means of expressing the emotion which Eliot had given me; secondly, because I wanted to test the resistance of my own language. Now that I look back after twelve years, I think that it was a rather useless effort from which I profited more than did the reader. It obliged me at least to dig up a fairly large field of English literature. I worked like a student, seven hours a day, for five or six months. I remember how much it tired me trying to discover whether the word "burning," with which the Fire Sermon ends, refers to Augustine or to Buddha. I am not sure whether I have ever discovered this. However, I recall the work I did with some nostalgia. It was the last time that I could give myself up to a literary work in a carefree way. Then came the disorders of the war. But, even among the disorders, Eliot remained for me, as I imagine he did for many — I am also thinking of the prematurely lost Sidney Keyes — one of the rare lights in a darkened world.

> I said to my soul, be still, and wait without hope
> For hope would be hope for the wrong thing; wait without love
> For love would be love of the wrong thing; there is yet faith.

LETTER TO A FOREIGN FRIEND

> But the faith and the love and the hope are all in the waiting.
> Wait without thought, for you are not ready for thought:
> So the darkness shall be the light, and the stillness the dancing.

These lines are related in my mind to the roar of the first Hurricanes in the Greek sky. The English friend who had lent the text to me was killed on our soil. They show, I think, the power and the weakness of those who are still trying to look upon human life with independence.

You will hardly expect me to comment on Eliot's work in this letter, nor is it my intention. I find that there have been too many commentaries already; they merely disturb the reader's attention and end up in remarks such as the following, which I happened to overhear: "Eliot is not a good poet, because he writes about the Tarot pack of cards without really knowing it." Of course, Eliot's experiences are complex. But why should we imagine them to be more complex than they are? For example, it has been said about the lines,

> The whole earth is our hospital
> Endowed by the ruined millionaire,

that the "ruined millionaire" is really Adam. Someone else would have said that he is the Zeus le Banquier of Gide. I would beg them not to force me to explain. I prefer these lines as they are written. The poet comes towards us with his own

[177]

experiences, and we go towards him, if we can, with our own. That is why I would tell the reader to enjoy the poetry of Eliot (I imitate the words he himself wrote about Shakespeare) with all the capacities he has for such enjoyment and with all the emotions he possesses, even though his feelings do not coincide entirely with those of Eliot. I would also advise him to try to follow the certain emergence of the poet in his search for life among all the perishable things which surround him: that sure road which begins in the garden of *La Figlia che Piange*, if you wish, and ends in the rose of "Little Gidding." I am not trying to simplify things which can't be simplified, but I, too, have strayed a great deal when trying to verify the details of Eliot's poetry, a thing which cannot always be done without doing damage to the poetry itself, and I think that when one has wasted much thought in trying to understand the meaning of "the redeeming from Time" by abstract analysis, it is worth asking oneself whether one could not have approached his meaning more directly by turning towards the experience of those moments when one has been struck by the emotion of love:

> There are hours when there seems to be no past and future
> Only a present moment of pointed light
> When you want to burn. When you stretch out your hand
> To the flames.

I would advise the reader to try to hear one of Mr. Eliot's *Quartets* in the same manner that he would go to hear the *Canzona di Ringraziamento* and to notice whether he does not feel, there also, the rise towards life of a wounded body. Here many distinctions would be needed. Let them be. But the dream of the old Mallarmé: *"Reprendre à la musique, le bien de la poésie"* (I am not sure if I remember the phrase correctly), which provoked so many aberrations and delusions, has been brought by Eliot far nearer to its realization than it has been by anyone else.

Along with the great services he has offered to poetry, I would like to add that we must not forget the integrity Eliot has, as an honest man, in his attitude both towards his art and towards himself and his fellow men. It is not a small thing when you remember that in these days there are poets who use the word "truth" or the word "freedom" with the same indifference with which they say to a stranger, "I am pleased to have met you," and that we have entered for good a period of mechanized stupidity, mechanized falsity and mechanized self-destruction. We have experienced some of these things in Greece, the fruits of contemporary inventions, and we pay dearly for them with our "blood and tears," as you used to say in the years of the war. I stop here. I would say bitter things and it is not the moment for them; however:

ON THE GREEK STYLE

> What is woven in the Councils of Princes
> Is woven also in our veins, our brains,
> Is woven like a pattern of living worms . . .

Let us continue our conversation. In those days when I first read these lines, a phrase of St. John of the Cross kept coming back to my mind, a small phrase that to me seemed to throw more light than a score of essays on the intangible poetic function: "He who learns the finest details of an art always goes forward in the dark and not with the initial knowledge, for, if he does not leave it behind him, he could never be liberated from it."

This phrase describes, in my opinion better than any other, the image I have of Eliot's progress. Not only because Eliot progressed in this way, discovering the finer details of his art, but also because it corresponds to the air of quiet and humble agony which this phrase gives out. In an age of overbearing pride that such a significant poet should be the poet of humility — is it not strange indeed? "Humility is endless."

I will make one final point. One morning in spring, roaming in the streets of Chelsea, I entered a deserted church — I cannot remember its name — to seek refuge from a sudden storm. From a stained-glass window I watched a tree struggling disheveled with the wind and the rain. Then, without any warning, suddenly the organ started playing, accompanying a solitary female voice, and then, after a few moments it stopped. I looked round me, there was no one there. Only the ornate tomb of Lord Dacre with the bodies of a man and a woman in stone on it, and the coat of arms with its motto: *Pour bien désirer.* "The empty chapel, the wind's home," I imagine, or the lost song, brought Eliot to my mind and I thought that one loved him *parce qu'il a bien désiré.*

Yours ever,
G.S.

X
On a Phrase of Pirandello

LE DIRECTEUR: *En attendant vous continuez de raisonner.*
LE PÈRE: *Parce que je souffre, Monsieur, je ne raisonne pas, j'explique ma souffrance.*

WE are apt to link together (and this not only on a special occasion as, for example, on hearing the news of Pirandello's death) those various intelligences that are outstanding and serve us as marks to show the way, lighthouses in this temporal archipelago where we live.

The show windows of noncommunicating forms that are the settings of the Sicilian playwright, where not one of all those characters in search of an author can ever fall into another's arms; that type of liminal character, known sometimes as Monsieur Teste, sometimes as La Jeune Parque, living enclosed in a cylinder of endless introspection; the incarcerated beings of F. H. Bradley, moving in the crystal prison of their senses, who so much attracted the poet Eliot — all these figures, each with its own idiosyncrasy and its own voice, may be, if one steps back a little and views them carefully, identified and seen to compose one single feature, the feature of a human type that emerged after the 1914 war and is already fading away be-

---
Written in 1937.

fore the vocal exuberancies of the various modern orthodoxies. This type of human being had (and still has) one or two outstanding characteristics: he is alone and divided; he has a highly trained logical faculty which dissolves his feelings and deprives him of the gift of oblivion. He has also the inescapable burden of wanting to know why and how he suffered.

This is what is described as the *après-guerre* type; people have called the whole era decadent, overintellectualized, scholastic, hydrocephalic. But however useful conventional words may sometimes be, it is a pity to use those ones which, solving no problems at all, give us the comfortable illusion that no problems exist. Beneath all this there was a sort of suffering in this situation, the deeper and the more explosive as the expressions overlying it are paradoxical, dry or disheartening. "I do not reason; I explain my pain away." This phrase would have been judged acceptable by Monsieur Teste, seeing, as he went to sleep, the geometry of his suffering; also by the poet who, without using this immediate expression, has formulated better than anyone else in his country what the English call "poignancy"; also by the surrealists, though they might have preferred to say, "We do not un-reason; we explain our pain away." However these last appear later; they mark a period of transition between the zone of loneliness and the zone of what Dante calls *bes-*

tialità, the period into which today we blindly move.

Moreover, the interdependence of the intellectual events of our times is something that deserves attention. I suppose that with most of us our intellectual background goes back at least sixty years, but still we must feel this interdependence, with many fluctuations, certainly, but with no interruption and with a persistence in its orientation which looks to us more sinister and fateful every day. A reaction against surroundings that are strange, an isolation, a feeling of suffocation as the life-giving forces of man dwindle, a search for human reality at whatever cost — this, in rough outline, might indicate some of the tendencies of the writer towards his surroundings in the period that leads us to the threshold of our own days in which the contemporary workers of the spirit begin to become "engaged." They are compelled, one should say, to become "engaged," because now, more than ever, the dilemma is inescapable: if you are not with me, you are against me. One could of course say that this dilemma has reference only to external matters and that the intellect cannot be subjugated to external matters. One should, however, reflect on the fact that those who have lived mentally within their times usually have a vivid experience of the tragic fate which has brought them to the limit of their endurance and of the tribulations which they have suffered either in person or through the bodies of their elder brothers. "I do not reason; I explain my pain away" (Pirandello). Or, "You see these living forms, this geometry of my suffering" (Valéry). "Thinking of the key, each confirms a prison" (Eliot). It is difficult for them to go back to these reasonings, this geometry, this prison.

"The Ivory tower should be rebuilt," said Paul Valéry not long ago at a banquet. And the critic who commented on these words added, "We ought to help those who refuse to surrender to the temporary elements of their time." I agree; but in an epoch where even the gods themselves have become orthodox and draw after them those who are most alive, I should like to know what we are going to do in this building. If an ivory tower is a colossal telescope through which "we are seen to be seeing" et cetera ad infinitum, I am afraid that such a multiplication would separate us even further from the eternal elements of this world, which, though they may end elsewhere can only have their beginnings in this world itself. And if "ivory tower" just means that the intellectual worker should do his work well, I cannot see why we should not call it, more prosaically, a workshop. I do not imagine that it means that we should sing of elephants or of the humpbacked oxen of Taratava, as was done so imperturbably by the Parnassian reaction. The only way of doing anything with this ivory tower —

ON A PHRASE OF PIRANDELLO

a place into which one is not retiring but being forced — would be to express both the tower itself and this coercion. This happened with Baudelaire. But such a thing must result in the collapse of the whole building. Because if Baudelaire gave birth to Mallarmé, and Mallarmé to Valéry, Baudelaire also gave birth to Rimbaud, who gave birth to *A Season in Hell* and many other things that are not ivory at all. Hate for the world that surrounds us and the love that ensues from this hate (or the opposite) cannot fit into this tower; there is not enough room. It can only accommodate a Parnassian imperturbability or a disintegrating sentimentality like *Mon âme est une enfante en robe de parade* Albert Samain).

After much quarreling we have arrived at the conclusion that the value of a work of art is not in what it is attempting to demonstrate, but in what it is. One can imagine a number of different ways in which this principle may be applied. One can imagine a state which obliges its intellectual workers to create works which will demonstrate its own particular "truths." Such a state will be fortunate, of course, if its artists are in a position to create works which "exist" independently of the truths that they are attempting to prove. We may also imagine a state that has so brought up its citizens that their works, by their existence alone, will demonstrate the eminence of that state and will thus declare its praise. It might even be possible to have no other works of art except these. We have examples of such states in our own ancient history and in the medieval period. But for such a state of affairs to come into being time is needed; the nourishment given by such a state has to be assimilated by many generations, so that all external pressure ceases to exist, and that the creator may ignore all that is extraneous to and disconnected with his own inner self. But however much we want to set things in order, we are bound to admit that a work, even if it supports the most vital truth in the world, is, unless it exists in itself, absolutely worthless. Furthermore, we are bound to admit that before a work comes to the point of "being," the creator must also have reached this point. Before we create, we must exist, as Goethe said. Whatever path we choose, there must always lie before us the problem of the existence, the reality, of the intellectual man. This existence, as a simple human being, will not come to us by means of the ivory tower. This existence, as an intellectual being, has not been afforded by the various political orthodoxies. We may reach it, perhaps, by the deep organic recognition of the necessity of saving, in our difficult times, whatever can be saved of human dignity.

XI

Art in Our Times

THE question was: what should an intellectual do in face of the religious fanaticisms unleashed by the political orthodoxies of the time? Those who have answered this question so far may, I think, be divided into two broad categories: (a) those who preferred to devote themselves to their work, believing, whether consciously or unconsciously, that their work itself could supply a better answer than they could themselves (some of these men were condemned to death by each of the opposing fanaticisms); and (b) those who opted — and I mean always as artists, and not as political beings — for one or the other of the existing camps of social struggle; political duty is no part of this discussion. The best among this latter group seem to me to have made their choice with complete awareness of what they were doing. That is to say they said to themselves perfectly clearly: "Today we are at war, and everything has to be subjugated to the orders of our commander in chief. Tomorrow, when the war is over, we shall have time for art." I must say that, inside this framework, I respect these men absolutely, since the only discussions that interest me are those where the par-

---

Written in 1945.

ticipants do not attempt to trouble the waters with demagogic contortions.

And in fact it is not logical to ask whether art should or should not be autonomous. Autonomy in art is an axiom. All we can ask is whether or not, in this tortured age in which we live, the artist is justified in deciding that art is a secondary matter and can be made dependent on the criteria and the success of some political opportunity. You see, in art, as in every other honest human activity, you cannot serve two masters, or, to quote Auden, who, however, served briefly in the Spanish Civil War:*

> Art is not life, and cannot be
> A midwife to society.
> [*New Year Letter*]

If the artist chooses to give his service to a political aim, I have nothing to say. For those, however, who have opted for art, I would add just a few more words.

When I speak of art, I am not in any way subscribing to the old theory of "Art for art's sake." This doctrine, which is now quite useless to all of us, finally came to mean the making of empty knickknacks by a handicapped man in a sterilized room. I mean only the intellectual order that has been created by good works of art, past and present, works that legislate and can teach. If we examine

---

* In fairness to Mr. Auden I should perhaps note that he has recently declared that the poems he wrote on the Spanish Civil War seem now to him to have been "trash." — G.S., 1966.

the conclusions that can be drawn from these works, we shall find that they are very far from being foreign to the struggles and the aspirations of their times. "The great artist," it has been said, "is not of his time; he is his time." And in fact the life of a poet — that conglomeration of impressions, emotions, reactions which are the material of his work — is also a part of the humanity that encompasses him with its own heartburnings, pains, grandeurs and humiliations. The more an artist is "true to himself" — and here I am thinking not so much of his superficial consciousness as of that knowledge that goes deep down to what is least known in human existence — the more completely will he instill his own time into his work. The bond between the artist and his time is not an intellectual one, not even the sentimental tie that may bring together two people in a political demonstration. It is rather the umbilical cord that connects mother and child, a purely biological attachment. "For we are conscripts to our age," said the poet whom I quoted previously. How else could it be? We all feed from the same messtin. And this explains why it is that we find that a true poet, who may subscribe to the most illogical and out-of-date political creed (in my humble opinion, political poetry, like poetical prose, is one of the most hideous things on earth), may produce work which, apart from its essential virtues, can be a better guide, even politically, to the thought of man than any number of public speakers.

But in order to work, the artist must be left free. Personally I hold the perhaps unusual view that one of the aims of the war, fought with such courage and so many sacrifices by our people, was just this kind of freedom — so that our country may be able to avoid falling into a state of cataleptic idiocy. And if, working in this way, as a free man, the poet happens to create some propaganda piece, as they call it (it might be, for example, *The Persians* of Aeschylus), this should not be regarded as a sign of wickedness, but rather as a work which necessarily, inevitably, and obligatorily demands the applause even of the writer's enemies.

To sum up: in holding this view which I believe to be, to the best of my judgment, the right one, I do not mean at all that the poet is an irresponsible being, constantly losing his balance at every impulse of his imagination or eccentricity. On the contrary my belief is that the solid artist is one of the most responsible beings on earth. He carries the burden of the responsibility of the struggle between life and death. Out of this human condition, in its madnesses and in its silences, what elements will he conserve? What must he conserve and what must he turn his back upon out of all this amorphous human material, which is terrifyingly alive and which follows him down the paths of sleep? "In dreams begins responsibility."

Author's Acknowledgements made in the First Edition

The author would like to thank Harcourt Brace Jovanovich, Inc., The Hogarth Press Ltd. and the author's Estate for permission to quote several poems from *The Complete Poems of Cavafy*, translated by Rae Dalven. Quotations from *Burnt Norton, The Waste Land, Marina, Ash Wednesday*, and *East Coker* are reprinted by permission of the publishers, Harcourt Brace Jovanovich, Inc. and Faber and Faber, Ltd., from *Collected Poems 1909-1962*, by T.S. Eliot.

The author is grateful to Edmund Keeley and Nanos Valaoritis for permission to reprint their translation of *Letter to a Foreign Friend*.

Biographical Note

George Seferis (the nom de plume of George Seferiades) was born in Smyrna in 1900, and moved to Athens with his family when he was fourteen. He studied in Paris at the end of the First World War and afterwards joined the Greek diplomatic service. From 1957 to 1962 he lived in London as Ambassador of Greece to the Court of St. James's. His first collection of poetry, *Turning Point,* was published in 1931, and was followed over the years by the publication of several other collections of both poetry and essays, which have been translated into many languages, and for which he was awarded the Nobel Prize. He died in Athens in 1971.